TURNAROUND

TURNAROUND

How twenty well-known companies came back from the brink

Edited by Rebecca Nelson
with
David Clutterbuck

MERCURY BOOKS
Published by W.H. Allen & Co. Plc

First published in 1988
by the Mercury Books Division of
W.H. Allen & Co. Plc
44 Hill Street, London W1X 8LB

Set in Concorde & Helvetica by Phoenix Photosetting
Printed and bound in Great Britain by
Mackays of Chatham Ltd, Chatham, Kent

British Library Cataloguing in Publication Data

Turnaround: how twenty well-known
   companies came back from the brink.
   1. Business firms. Profits. Improvement
   I. Nelson, Rebecca   II. Clutterbuck,
   David, *1947—*
   658.1'554

   ISBN 1–85251–090–0

CONTENTS

FOREWORD

by David Clutterbuck

Companies are like people. Their mortality rate tends to be relatively high in the first few years of life and as they pass from mature middle age. During the latter period they sicken but they may recover. Those that don't recover may go out in a blaze of bankruptcy or simply wither away over a period of years.

Every business goes through several stages of growth and transition. The most difficult perhaps is the transition from an entrepreneurially managed company, where the founder and his personality are central to everything that happens, to a professionally managed operation, where teamwork becomes more important than personal genius. The organisation calls for a different type of leader, a consolidator, who will bring together the disparate elements of a business that has grown in large part by feel and intuition and weld them into a business that grows by the steady virtues of planning, controls and systems.

The chances of surviving this transition are greatly improved if the founder has the courage to allow it to happen before he quits the business or dies. Such was the case of the founder of a major furniture retailer who recognised his own entrepreneurial strengths and his weakness as a consolidator. Fairly early on in the company's history he backed away from general management into new product innovation, leaving the day-to-day running of the company in the hands of professional managers. This case illustrates that an effective consolidator does not stop growth, he merely brings it under tighter control. The opposite can be seen in the case of a major West Country engineering group, whose founder held the helm firmly until he died. His successor was chosen from a team that had learnt over decades to say yes to the founding genius and to defer to his drive and ingenuity while sublimating its own. Unable to question the way things were done before, the team members continued as they had always done and the opportunity for growth-oriented change was lost. Progressive decline was inevitable, and so it is proving.

The next major crisis in a company's life tends to come when a long-serving consolidator or a succession of consolidators succeeds too well. By systematising and ordering he stifles the ingenuity and initiative of the original company. These are not bad managers on the whole, but their very success at managing rather than leading changes the nature of the organisation in one of two ways. The first is that the company becomes increasingly rigid in its structures, attitudes and ways of doing things. It develops an insensitivity to changes in the external world and an atmosphere of being a comfortable place to work. The sense of urgency so noticeable in the vibrant, growth-oriented company is absent. The second is that conservatism becomes the underlying principle of all decisions. In the worst cases this leads to increasingly centralised bureaucracy, vast mausoleum-like corporate headquarters and a total isolation of the top management from what happens at the dirty end of the business.

For the badly managed company, the crisis tends to come from poor trading results. For well managed companies, the crisis is more likely to be an unwanted takeover bid. A good example of the latter may be Sears Holdings, one of the most conservatively managed companies in Europe. Sears has delivered solid results for more than 10 years since the death of Sir Charles Clore, the entrepreneur who brought the group together. It has also grown steadily and has continued to amass an enviable property portfolio. But the simple fact that it is a company which has had a lengthy period of consolidator leadership means that it is perceived by much of the stock market as unimaginative, uninspired and underutilising its resources. The wolves have gathered and, barring a change in leadership style, will have their meal eventually.

This book is not concerned with companies like Sears, which are healthy by almost any standards, but with those that have passed through the crisis of financial disaster. Not all the cases in the book are companies that have been on the edge of bankruptcy, but all have been forced to accept that their survival depended upon radical change and all have had the courage to make change happen.

One of the most profound studies of corporate turnarounds in recent years comes in *Corporate Recovery* (Penguin, 1984), by Stuart Slatter of the London Business School. Slatter lists ten key elements of successful recovery strategies. The first of these, and in our view frequently the most important, is the appointment of a new chief executive. While not every turnaround requires a change of leadership, it is certainly easier in most cases for a new leader to convince people in the organisation that from now on things are going to be done differently. The new broom is also less likely to respect old loyalties and sacred cows, which may need to be swept aside before effective action can be taken.

That a change in leadership is so often necessary is indicated by the reasons the crisis came about in the first place. A survey of chief executives in the United States found that more than half of them ascribed failure to 'internally generated problems within management's control' – in other words, poor management. In such circumstances those who led the company into its crisis are probably the last people to admit to the seriousness of the situation and to assess the remedial actions needed.

Our cases illustrate some of the qualities required by the crisis or transitional leader. He must have a very clear idea of what has to be done to save the company and why. He must be a good communicator, to convince others that, even if he is not right, he should be given the benefit of the doubt and loyal commitment. (This may be the hardest task of all in an organisation where the employees have lost faith in management's ability to lead.) He must be a superb delegator, for to try and do everything himself will only force him back on to the tramlines followed by his predecessor. As a delegator, one of his greatest weapons is his infectious enthusiasm, and he must have a remarkable amount of sheer guts and determination to see his vision through. The strange thing is that these extraordinary people may in reality be quite ordinary – perhaps this is in part what makes them so believable.

The second of Slatter's elements of a turnaround strategy is the imposition of strong financial control. It may seem strange that a bureaucratic company may be weak in this area, but in practice such companies have so many controls that financial control is weakened. By focusing on finance rather than other forms of control, the crisis leader stems the bleeding – the first and most critical step in gaining control of the operation as a whole. Cutting the costs of the operation is equally important: this requires not merely wiping out overheads, such as oversized company headquarters and staff functions, but seeking ways of increasing margins at every step of the sales–manufacture–delivery process. Stemming the bleeding may also mean disposing of some of the assets – a tough decision when, for example, the most profitable division has to be sold off to raise survival capital for the rest of the organisation.

Slatter also lists organisational change and decentralisation. Again, this is clearly reflected in our case studies, where increased autonomy has been an essential part of the drive to bring operating units closer to their customers.

The new leader also looks closely at the company's products and the markets they serve. The most frequent cause for company failure is purely and simply not giving the customer what he or she wants. Reassessing the market and its needs is a longer-term action than tightening financial control, but it is equally critical. From this assessment come changes in how the company manufactures its products or provides its service, how it distributes and how it sells.

The last three elements noted by Slatter are debt restructuring (persuading investors and creditors to exchange debt for equity, for example) to reduce the company's debt/equity ratio; attracting additional investment; and acquisition. The last mentioned, adopted with particular success by two of our case studies, Aer Lingus and Waterford, is mainly a weapon for companies that are stagnating rather than passing through a financial crisis, but it has a number of attractions. It may, for example, take the company rapidly into areas of significant market growth, or it may allow economies of scale that raise margins. This is a high-risk strategy, however, for if the acquisition also turns out to be a lacklustre performer, the company has made its original problems worse while simultaneously saddling itself with increased debt.

Most of these elements occur in some or all of our case studies, which are drawn from both Britain and Europe and from a wide spectrum of manufacturing and service industries. There is also considerable variation in the degree of crisis encountered and the size of the companies concerned.

The following observations can be drawn from these examples. However deep the crises the companies found themselves in, the basic businesses were still sound. Most of them got into difficulties because they were either insufficiently aware of what was happening in their own organisation or in their markets. But amidst their obvious (at least to an outsider and in hindsight) weaknesses were clear strengths on which the turnaround manager could build. At British Airways the strengths included the extensive route network; at Waterford, the craftsmanship and international reputation of a quality manufacturer; and Vickers, engineering excellence. These strengths provided a starting point, an island of stability amidst shifting sands of change, that both enabled investors to see the core worth of the company and gave employees the psychological reassurance that they could not have been doing every-thing wrong.

Most of the turnarounds followed a discernible pattern. The initial stage comprised a mixture of assessment and action, with the chief executive taking painful decisions on usually partial evidence. There simply wasn't the time to conduct detailed deliberations. If the patient had gangrene, then the limb had to be amputated first before more subtle medications could be expected to work. In some cases, such as Acorn, this meant dispensing with nearly half the workforce in a very short period. For Enka, it also meant a freeze on investment. However severe the cut-backs, they had one basic aim – giving the company a financial breathing space in which it could begin to plan for a more confident future.

Many of our turnaround companies stress the importance of commu-nication at this stage. To carry the remaining staff with him, and to prevent panic setting in, the chief executive has to share his sense of purpose with them. Communication is equally important at the second stage, where control over the financial bleeding has been re-established and it is now possible to focus on medium-term rather than immediate survival objectives. In this phase the chief executive begins to create a cohesive team around himself. He is less concerned with forcing people to take decisive actions they should have taken months or years earlier than with identifying the path forward. The team may not be the same as when he started. The reactions of the senior managers during the first stage of turnaround will have shown him those who can contribute to the subsequent phases and those who will hinder progress.

The new team undertakes a process of exploration and questioning. Its members may well 'zero-base' everything the company does in an effort to identify whether it is producing the right products or services for the right markets. They return to the basic questions: 'What businesses are we in?', 'What businesses should we be in?', 'What do our customers want?', 'How can we give it to them in the most cost-effective manner?'

The answers to those questions allow strategic decisions to be made for both the medium and long term. Parts of the business may have to be sold off to raise capital for expansion in the areas where the company foresees opportunities for greater growth and profitability. Investments must be made, new skills acquired, and new products developed.

Although most turnarounds comprised much the same elements, the difference in circumstances dictated that each of the companies stressed one or more critical elements on which to focus the third, implemen-tation stage. For British Airways and SAS, it was customer care; for

Italtel, innovation; for UDT, investment in technology; for IRI, privatisation; and for Enka, specialisation in high value-added market niches.

In most cases the medium-term strategy consisted of a concentration of effort and resources on the core business or businesses – on sticking to the last. Peripheral operations that did not contribute significantly to the main business were divested, both to raise cash and to prevent top management wasting time on anything that didn't directly relate to the health of the core.

The final stage in the typical successful turnaround is the expansion stage. Having got the finances under control, achieved a focus of activity in a small number of healthy operations that are either stable or growing, the company starts to look to the long term. Its basic strategy has already been set, so that all it needs now are the opportunities to move them forward at a faster rate. It may do so by heavy investment in key areas, as with Enka and Fiat, or by acquisition or by both, as with British Airways, whose bid to take over Caledonian was fully in tune with the expansion phase of a turnaround company.

All this takes time, usually a minimum of 5 years for a company of significant size. By and large the companies in this book are either in the third stage or just entering the fourth. It is here that the greatest danger may lie. For one thing, the turnaround leader may not be the most suitable leader for the next phase of growth. Depending on the kind of strategy to be pursued, he may be so enamoured of the management of crisis that he is incapable of communicating the messages needed in a company aiming for stable growth. Like Mao and the Cultural Revolution, he may become greatly frustrated without the daily injection of adrenalin that comes from managing in a crisis mode.

Another danger at this time is that the company may simply repeat the mistakes of its past. Guinness, for example (not one of the cases in this book), made a great deal of noise about how it had divested peripheral businesses in turning round a lacklustre performance. Yet having put the company to rights, the new management immediately set about another spree of buying anything in sight.

Among the lessons learned by the Swedish Statsforetag, the national body that takes over companies that the state wishes to preserve from bankruptcy, is that turnaround is not a once and for all phenomenon and that a company that intends to survive in the long term must go through all three turnaround stages. Very often companies hit by a major crisis respond by doing all the things required in stage one. They cut costs, arrange refinancing, cut out all the fat in the organisation and return to profitability. Yet if they fail to carry out a fundamental reassessment of their business and fail to implement a coherent strategy of *preventing future crises*, they are highly likely to be caught out by the next downturn in the business cycle. This time they have fewer reserves, there is little or no fat to cut and therefore the period between the warning of crisis and the depth of the crisis is much shorter. By the time the management reacts, it may be too late.

All too often it is indeed too late. According to strategist W. Stewart Howe, in the ten years 1967 to 1976 some 9 per cent of the United States' most important companies underwent a turnaround – defined in this case as an 80 per cent or more drop in earnings, followed by recovery. But for every company that recovered, two more failed to make it. The statistics for the UK are unlikely to be different.

In many cases the stories of these turnarounds are presented in the words of the executives responsible. While it could fairly be said that the authors will not have an entirely unbiased view of what happened, it is in every case their perception of and commitment to what had to be done and how it should be done that has enabled the company to restore its fortunes. We therefore believe that the experience of these executives will be of at least some help to others who have the responsibility of crisis leadership thrust upon them.

1 British Airways

by Sir Colin Marshall,
Chief Executive, BRITISH AIRWAYS

A number of commentators looking at the results and achievements of British Airways over the past few years have described our turnaround as 'miraculous'. No doubt the term was kindly meant. However, I prefer to think that our success is capable of rational analysis.

Success in business is something that has to be built up step by step, by a combination of hard thinking and hard work, usually in that order. Inevitably it takes time.

The problems that British Airways faced in the early 1980s were largely the consequences of a politically inspired merger in the early 1970s between two state-owned airlines, British European Airways and British Overseas Airways. However worthy the objects of that merger, the practical results were unhappy ones.

The combined organisation was grossly overstaffed, morale had largely collapsed as two workforces reared in different cultures were forced unwillingly into a marriage of convenience, and customer service standards declined as the management's energies were expended on fighting a series of internal crises. Employee relations, in particular, deteriorated to the stage where, on the then management's own evidence, there were some forty different industrial disputes going on within the airline at one time. Some or all of those problems might have been overcome in time, but an industry-wide recession at the beginning of the 1970s brought about a financial crisis that threatened the airline's ability to survive.

One reason was that British Airways was in a classic poverty trap. It was seriously under-capitalised and its modest profit levels were quite inadequate as a source of self-generated capital. As a result it was obliged to borrow ever-increasing sums to finance the new aircraft and equipment it needed if it was to remain competitive. Inevitably the meagre profits, which should have been reinvested in the business, were swallowed up in paying ever-increasing interest charges.

It was at this point, at the beginning of 1981, that Lord King became Chairman. His long-term remit from the Government, as the then owner of the business, was to prepare the airline for privatisation. In the event his immediate task, and that of the new management he brought in, was to save it from bankruptcy.

The steps he took at that time were tough but effective. Staff numbers were cut by 23,000, or about 40 per cent, unprofitable routes and obsolete aircraft were axed, and several hundred million pounds were written off in reducing to realistic levels the book value of ageing assets and providing for the severance costs of the excess staff.

If the medicine was strong, the effects were nonetheless salutary. It very quickly became apparent that, once freed from the burden of superfluous staff and unprofitable operations, the basic operation was capable of earning much higher profits than most people had believed possible. Although it was still labouring under a very large burden of capital debt, British Airways began to return healthy profits from which to reduce that burden and build its future prosperity.

It was a start, but it was a very long way from a recipe for success. Short-term financial disaster had been averted, but the airline still had to find a course that would lead it to long-term commercial success in an increasingly competitive environment. To chart that path, and to make sure we followed it, became one of my principal tasks after I joined British Airways on 1 February 1983.

The real problem, which very quickly became apparent as I started to learn my way around British Airways in those early days, was basically quite easy to identify. The airline had forgotten that it was a service industry.

There was nothing fundamentally wrong with its operation. It had an excellent route network, its aircraft were carefully maintained and expertly flown, and it possessed, even after the staff cuts, a large workforce of competent and dedicated people. If lifting people off the ground in one place and putting them down again safely somewhere else had been enough to ensure success (and a number of senior British Airways managers had grown accustomed to that concept), then British Airways might have been accounted a successful airline.

It was not enough, however. The truth was that a disturbingly high proportion of British Airways' customers in those days flew with us because they had to, not because they wanted to. They lost no opportunity of saying so, especially to their friends.

Horror stories abounded. Passengers complained of grubby uncared-for aircraft, while cabin crews in turn told tales of woe about broken meal trolleys and ovens that would not heat the meals.

The complaints about our staff were, if anything, even worse. In fact I am sure that the great majority of staff did their utmost to look after the customers as well as they could, but our passengers, being human, tended to forget the good and remember the unhappy experiences.

Many of the staff, particularly those in contact with the customer, were undoubtedly cynical and frustrated after years of being urged from a great height to do a good job, and then denied the means of doing it. There were too many cases of a cabin crew boarding an aircraft to find that the broken oven they had reported on the same aircraft 3 weeks before was still there – and still broken!

One of the most important tasks in any service business is to keep what I will call the 'shine' on the product day in and day out. It demands an unremitting attention to detail, which in itself can be very expensive in management time, and also requires a firm sense of priorities when it comes to spending money.

There is a natural but very dangerous temptation, particularly when a company is facing cash-flow problems, for the management to persuade itself that it can cut back just a little on the standard of cabin cleaning, or the quality of the in-flight catering, or the issue of replacement uniforms, and the customers will never notice. The first time round, they possibly don't. The second or third or fourth time, they do. Too late the management discovers that it has destroyed in weeks or months a reputation that took decades to build.

We discovered all these problems, and more, when we started to tackle some of the more glaring deficiencies. For the most part they were straightforward management problems, and we tackled them at the right end – by making senior managers go out in person and put things right.

We sought to avoid the traditional hierarchical approach to problem-solving in the airline, in which the task was handed down from A to B to C. This new approach meant injecting a commitment to personal accountability that in many departments had been lacking for too long.

For instance, we gave one manager the specific task of getting the interiors of our aircraft clean. We also gave him the authority to cut across all the established lines of authority in order to get the job done. In fact he had to tread on very few toes, for once the senior line management knew what was expected of them, and understood that we wanted excellence, not excuses, remarkable things began to happen.

Junior airport staff, many of whom had never seen an executive above the level of their immediate supervisor, became accustomed to the sight of very senior managers indeed climbing aboard aircraft at 6 o'clock in the morning to make sure cabins were spotless and galleys were clean and in working order before the first service of the day took off.

As our cash flow position improved, we began to spend large sums on all the basic things that had been neglected for years: passenger seats, carpets, catering equipment, ground vehicles. It was a very long list.

These highly visible improvements were not lost on the passengers, who for the first time in years saw evidence that we were paying them the compliment of caring whether they enjoyed their flight, and of wanting them to come back again.

The story of Super Shuttle is worth recounting, because it encapsulated everything we were trying to do to win our customers' goodwill.

The existing Shuttle service on our key domestic routes to destinations such as Glasgow, Edinburgh, Belfast and Manchester was technically very successful, because it gave business travellers the convenient, high-frequency service they needed. What it did not offer them was any semblance of personal care.

In pursuit of simplicity and low costs the airline had always set its face against any kind of in-flight service at all. While that might have been good accounting practice, it was not the way to win the custom of a hungry businessman, compelled to start a long day by flying to Scotland at 7 o'clock in the morning with no breakfast and not even the offer of a cup of coffee.

That take-it-or-leave-it attitude was sustainable as long as we had no competition. But the day a competitor appeared on the route and offered a full hot meal, our hungry passengers voted with their stomachs. In an alarmingly short space of time we lost nearly 30 per cent of our market, with every reason to suppose that if we did not react, we would lose a great deal more. The whole Shuttle concept was in jeopardy.

After extensive consumer research, we determined that the problem, in a word, was breakfast. Provided they were not asked to fly unfed on an early morning service, the great majority of passengers would prefer the Shuttle to its competitor every time.

That told us all we needed to know. We abandoned the old 'no catering' rule, and started offering all our early morning passengers a full hot breakfast except on the short flights to Manchester, on which continental breakfast was supplied, with a choice of morning papers for good measure. The customers responded enthusiastically, we won back a large measure of the business we had lost, and the Super Shuttle concept has never looked back.

Napoleon said that in war morale outweighs material factors by three to one. He would have made a good manager in a service industry; for clearly all the material benefits that were flowing through from our improved financial position were going to be of no use without a complete change of attitude on the part of many of our staff.

There was little point in operating a smartly refurbished aircraft if the passengers were looked after by a surly and demoralised crew. Why should our customers be expected to believe that British Airways had changed for the better before the people who worked for British Airways believed it themselves?

There were also some yawning gulfs that needed to be bridged. They not only lay between staff and management, but also between staff in different departments, often with totally different backgrounds and experience.

We invited about a third of the entire airline staff, the people at all levels who came into contact with the customer, to go through a two-day course called 'Putting People First'. In it, we set out to show people how their own attitudes towards the customer, and towards their own colleagues, in turn affected the way in which their customers saw them. It was simple, understandable and convincing, and as we had expected, suspicion soon turned to enthusiasm among the thousands of staff who took the course.

By the time that the first phase of 'Putting People First' had been completed, the course was being paid a rare compliment. The staff who had not been included in the original programme because they were not in direct contact with the customers began to complain at being left out!

That problem at least was easy to solve: we organised a related course for them as well, for the benefit to staff morale greatly outweighed the marginal extra cost. From there we moved logically into a whole range of new training initiatives.

It is self-evident, one might think, that the staff of a large organisation must work as a team. But since a large organisation like ours is also very complicated, and employs a large number of diverse skills, that is more easily said than done.

We had already found that a great many people in the airline, particularly the younger staff, had no idea what other departments did, or why their work was important. Very often they did not even know what their own jobs contributed to the end result.

We therefore devised a simple programme called 'A Day in the Life', in which mixed groups of staff, drawn from right across the airline, spent a day in a lively and entertaining exhibition run by their own colleagues in other departments, with real working exhibits and experts from those departments on hand to explain how they worked and why they mattered to the airline. It was a revelation to most of the staff who took part in it, and it was so successful that when we came to sell shares in British Airways in February 1987, we used the same basic show to tell City financial experts about British Airways. Many of them voted it the most interesting company presentation they had ever seen.

Staff motivation had to go hand in hand with the next development we were planning, which was a complete change in the airline's appearance, designed to emphasise a clean break with the past. The first stage was a completely new external livery for our aircraft. It was designed for us by a leading specialist in the field, Landor Associates, and it introduced a completely new range of corporate colours – red, blue and silver. We introduced it in a series of spectacular presentations to our own staff, and the warmth of their own response was an encouraging augury of the way in which the general public was to receive it.

We were working simultaneously on a range of other design changes, including new uniforms and workwear for our staff and a completely new decor for our travel shops and airport lounges worldwide.

Inevitably these changes took a considerable time to introduce, for in an organisation of our size the logistics of such a change are formidable. We had to repaint over 150 aircraft, dress over 28,000 staff – about three-quarters of the entire payroll – in new clothing, and undertake refurbishment of Executive Club lounges and nearly 200 travel shops. The aircraft and the staff uniforms were virtually finished by the summer of 1987, and refurbishment of the Executive Club lounges is well under way. The travel shops will take longer to refurbish completely, although the task of fitting them with new external fascias is complete.

It is always hard to say at what point in the life of a threatened company the rescue process ceases and normal day-to-day management functions take over. In our case the process of change has never stopped and never will, if only because in an intensely competitive environment like ours we can never take anything for granted.

An airline which says, for instance, 'We have the best reservations system (or catering, or passenger check-in, or anything else) in the world and no improvement is needed' is heading for a disagreeable shock, because somebody, somewhere, is planning to steal a march on it. The only way to keep ahead is to continue to improve our service and raise our standards.

That is why, to take a couple of examples, we have spent some £60 million in completely re-equipping the interiors of our 747 fleet to bring it up to the standards of the best of our competitors, and a further £25m on our new Club Europe and Club World products. These are designed to appeal especially to the business travellers who form such an important part of our traffic, both to the Continent and further afield.

Throughout the years of change one of our objectives has been to render British Airways what I will call financially stormproof. Back in the 1970s the airline had been just about capable of staying afloat financially so long as it sailed in calm waters. But when an economic storm blew up, its frail profitability vanished and it rapidly began to sink beneath the burden of its own costs. Those costs were not only too high, but there was no machinery by which the airline could shed them rapidly to cope with a severe recession. We had to make sure that that situation could never recur.

Our new-found resilience was put to the test in the early summer of 1986, when what had looked like being a buoyant year turned very rapidly into a potential disaster. Beneath the twin impacts of international terrorism and the nuclear accident at Chernobyl our transatlantic business melted away.

Thanks to an imaginative, aggressive and highly successful marketing campaign we were able to restore the situation and weather the storm much better than most of our competitors – so much so that we ended the year with a satisfactory profit. But the episode illustrated how easily the economic climate in which we operate could turn chilly almost overnight.

The key to survival in situations like this is flexibility, and two examples of the kind of flexibility we have achieved will suffice.

We have pioneered the principle of operating leases for our aircraft. Put very simply, this means that many of our aircraft in service or on order are owned by financial consortia, and leased by us on terms that permit us the freedom either to renew or terminate the agreement at prearranged intervals. This means that we can acquire new aircraft in a way that enables us to adjust our fleet at relatively short notice to meet changing market demands, instead of being obliged to commit ourselves to long-term capital investment decisions.

Flexibility in staff numbers is equally important, and we have broken new ground in this field, too. We now have a nucleus of full-time air cabin crew who provide the essential year-round staffing levels, and we supplement them with a substantial number of what we call support cabin crew. These staff are trained to exactly the same high standard as all our crews, but instead of being employed full-time they are called in as required to meet the varying needs of different routes at different times of year.

The benefit in both cases is essentially the same. It enables us to step up our aircraft capacity when demand is buoyant, and step it down again relatively quickly and cheaply if and when patterns of demand start to change. This is the kind of thinking that must guide all our decisions from now on, and much of our effort has been geared to constructing the kind of management that can visualise the problem in those terms.

There has been, I repeat, nothing miraculous in our turnaround over the past few years. We simply brought to bear the basic management qualities of clear thinking, commonsense and leadership, guided of course by a very clear mental picture of what we wanted to achieve. If a company is capable of being saved, then those qualities, together with a generous measure of hard work, are surely the only sound prescription for success.

2 The Waterford Glass Group

by Jane Wynn, Deputy Editor,
Financial Weekly

When the chief executive of Ford of Ireland was asked if he would like to take the top job at Waterford Glass, he was, he admits, 'not terribly enthusiastic'. The name of Waterford was revered by every son and daughter of Ireland. It symbolised beauty, elegance and success. But the recent history of the company had been far from sparkling.

Paddy Hayes, the executive in question, had worked for Ford for 30 years, 14 of these as executive head of the company. He had earned a reputation for being a tough but fair manager and had a high standing in the Irish business community.

His reaction to the invitation to join Waterford was to ask himself why he should want to leave a nice, safe, prestigious job at the age of 53 and put that reputation on the line. He rejected the offer. But then he began to reflect on what challenges lay ahead for him between the years of 54 and 65. Waterford represented an opportunity to do something very substantial. He changed his mind and early in 1985 became chairman and chief executive of the Waterford Glass Group. He had every reason to face his first day with trepidation.

Waterford crystal had never lost the devotion of Irishmen nor of Waterford's customers throughout the world. But while the reputation of the product remained untarnished, the business performance of the company did not. It had turned in several years of pedestrian performance. For many years effectively owned by the McGrath family, it had succumbed to many of the negative traits of family-run companies.

But in 1984 Waterford underwent a fundamental change of ownership. Globe Investment Trust, the largest UK investment trust, bought the 21.6 per cent stake from the McGrath family. The members of the founding family resigned from the board and two Globe directors joined it. It was Globe who approached Paddy Hayes.

In less than 2 years Waterford was transformed. It had developed a strategy that had all the clarity and definition of the finest cut crystal. It had built a new management team, a healthy balance sheet, made a successful rights issue in the United States, become a more fashionable name on the visiting lists of top City brokers and was about to make an acquisition which would make it a world leader in luxury tabletop ware. In short, it was anything but a medium-sized obscure Irish company.

The rescuing white knight is a role Hayes was to play again later when Waterford acquired Wedgwood. When he came to Waterford he was very much the questing knight. He was searching for a strategy that would turn Waterford into a major world player.

But he did far more than merely remove a few cobwebs that had accumulated to dull the sparkle of the crystalware company. He took a long hard look at the products that were on the Waterford table.

Hayes was determined to make Waterford's most marketable assets – its handcrafted crystalware and Aynsley fine bone china (later the subject of a management buy-out) – the leading edge products of the company. He knew these core products could be marketed more widely throughout the world, and that if the company was given a fresh business direction, it would not only be more profitable but would have a base to do something even more exciting.

That opportunity, in the form of Wedgwood, arrived a little sooner than Hayes had expected. But it was a once in a lifetime chance which he and his management team were able to grasp with both hands because they had done the groundwork at Waterford. They were in a position to be able to claim they could work the same turnaround magic on Wedgwood they had already worked on Waterford.

Hayes is a quietly spoken Irishman. He is charming but direct, and the modesty with which he now speaks about the Waterford turnaround belies the swift determination with which he acted.

'It was obvious we had to get rid of the non-performing peripheral businesses. We had to "stick to our knitting", as they say. We were lucky because it was not only obvious, it was also fashionable. So we did it.'

The non-performing businesses had been quickly identified as a serious drain on the group's performance. They were not only contributing to a highly geared balance sheet, they were also a distraction from the core expertise of the company – the Waterford crystal and the Aynsley china.

Today a visitor to the main glassworks will see row upon row of glassblowers and cutters fashioning each article by hand. The teams of apprentices, craftsmen and masters zealously guard the traditional crafts of Waterford. It is these crafts which give Waterford the exclusivity that is its trademark throughout the world.

One of the achievements of Hayes was to build a company which, although founded upon the oldest labour-intensive methods, is in fact a modern *business* force. But in order to preserve these skills and make Waterford a leading, cost-effective world manufacturing force Paddy Hayes had to persuade the company to change both its culture and its business profile. He tackled head-on areas of the group that before his arrival had been regarded as sacrosanct.

Until the arrival of Hayes, Waterford had been predominantly owned by the McGrath family. Their claim to fame was that in the 1950s they saw the opportunity for re-establishing the manufacture of glassware in Ireland. But in the 1970s, the halcyon days of the Irish economy, they had been influenced by a fashion which affected many other businesses – diversification. The company made one very successful acquisition in 1970. It bought Aynsley China, of Stoke-on-Trent. Gripped by the diversification craze that followed Ireland's entry into the EEC, however, it bought into other home-based businesses – the Switzer department store group, the Smith Group (Renault distributors in Ireland) and the John Hinde printing company.

The John Hinde company is still in the Waterford Group and is steadily profitable but the other two businesses were eating away at management time and resources. This is illustrated by the following figures. In 1985 Waterford and Aynsley accounted for 49 per cent of net sales totalling IR£125m and contributed 93 per cent of operating income. In contrast, Switzers and Smiths accounted for negligible income generation. On 23 per cent of sales, Switzers produced 3 per cent of income and the Smith Group gave a tiny 2 per cent of income on 26 per cent of sales.

'I think,' says Hayes, 'the McGraths were very paternalistic. They did not want to sell anything they had bought. It was not considered good for Ireland to sell part of the Waterford Glass Group. Their philosophy was to hold on and hope it came good.'

When Hayes arrived at Waterford, a day he can still recall vividly, he recognised a classic turnaround situation. The company had lost its direction and management time was being wasted on peripheral interests that he knew would continue to eat away at the company's cash unless they were sold.

On that first day Hayes remembers feeling very lonely. 'I even asked myself, where do I go?' It was a question he was to ask about the company. The answer was not long in coming. By November of that year he had drawn up a 5-year corporate plan setting out key strategic aims.

The style of management which would implement the plan was much influenced by Hayes himself. Highly respected in the Irish business community, and now in the UK and the States also, he is a man who is regarded as something of a loner. A firm teetotaller, he has claimed never to have bought a round in his life. He prefers to sip mineral water from a Waterford crystal goblet and discuss his great passion, opera.

The loner has an important asset. He is able to stand back from the crowd and take an overview. This is what Hayes did. He looked at what he calls the big picture. Just as he has a passion for opera and speaks with deep-felt admiration for the beauty of the Waterford crystal, he is a man of vision.

His vision for Waterford was to see that a profitable and debt-free Waterford could become a major player on the world stage. He was able to bring his team with him because in stepping back from the company, an advantage he had as an outsider, he could present a future that was different but feasible. He is also a good team-builder. There is a visible flow of ideas between him and his executive team, and, just as important, a sense of fun and commitment.

'I spent a great deal of time talking and being very careful,' he remembers. 'I knew I would be a great culture shock. The company had moved with my arrival from a part-time, somewhat benevolent chairman to a full-time executive chairman.' Those first few weeks of exploring the new territory and getting to know the people were to be repeated within a short time after the acquisition of Wedgwood.

Hayes constructed a board that he is proud of. It consists of four non-executive directors; as well as two members of Globe Investment Trust; his finance director, Anthony Brophy; the new chief executive of Aynsley, Geoffrey Deith; a new sales and marketing director, Redmond O'Donoghue; and Gerry Demsey, Patrick Byrne and Colm O'Connell. It was this team which, with some outstanding people from the existing management team – for example, Colm O'Connell, who is managing director of Waterford Crystal, and general manager Billy Power – drew up the all-important 5-year corporate plan. Paddy Hayes summarised their strategy as it was before the acquisition of Wedgwood as follows: 'To increase production of Waterford Crystal and Aynsley China in combination with an international marketing drive, to reduce debt levels following reorganisation of our existing business and to rationalise loss-making operations'.

'Once we had decided what to do,' he says, 'no one had any trouble at all in doing it.'

By December 1985 a deal had been arranged with the House of Fraser to buy Waterford's 60 per cent stake in Switzer and Company. The IR£7m sale had the immediate effect of reducing Waterford's net borrowings by IR£10.5m.

At the end of 1983 net debt had been at an all-time high of IR£47m, but by the end of 1985 this had come down by 61 per cent to IR£18m. Indeed by the time interim results were announced in February 1986 pre-tax profits were up 27 per cent to IR£18.5m on a turnover up by 4.1 per cent. The share price had already risen dramatically from 48p to 120p.

The sale of the Smith Group, the Renault dealer network, took a little longer. It was losing money and needed heavy rationalisation. Waterford closed some of the company-owned dealerships and sub-let half the remaining fourteen garages to owner operators. In 1986 the company sold Smith's to an Irish businessman for a nominal sum.

Paddy Hayes said: 'The disposal is a major step in Waterford's policy of concentration on the core crystal and china businesses. We fought hard to ensure the Smith Group had a good home and I believe we have concluded a deal which will ensure a sound future for the Renault franchise in Ireland.'

Ironically, when Hayes was appointed as Waterford's chief, many people said it was because of his experience with Ford which could be used to turn around the Smith business. But in Hayes' mind there has never been any doubt that the Smith Group would have to go. It was not central to Waterford's strategy and was in a business area which Hayes perceived as being on the wane.

The sale reduced net debt by IR£7.2m and bills by IR£11.8m. But for Hayes this was by no means far enough. He was determined to bring borrowing down to zero. 'It was an obsession,' he says. 'I believed if we could get borrowings down to nothing we could do something new and very exciting.'

Hayes was now faced with another, perhaps more intractable, problem to solve, i.e. inventory levels. Waterford has as many as 2,000 products and about 80 per cent are exported and stocks kept in warehouses around the world.

High stock levels tie up capital and inflate company borrowings. This can be seen by the level of inventories in 1983, which had soared to more than 60 per cent of total sales. This in turn exerted an unhealthy pressure on interest charges. Hayes determined to attack stock levels. This was an essential part of the corporate plan. His aim was 'never to have more or less than three months' supply of any item in any market, at any time'.

In effect, this had fundamental implications for the company's marketing policy. The way to cut down the crystal mountain was to increase sales faster than production. Distribution channels around the world had to be streamlined and co-ordinated with customer demand. Waterford had to become a market-led rather than a production-pushed company.

Improving inventory control necessitated a much finer tuning to market demand. In order to run stocks more efficiently stock levels had to be reduced and at the same time the product mix had to change. One of the things Waterford did in the States was to control stock and production by computer information systems for their retailers. The result was that by mid-1986 stock levels in the United States had been reduced dramatically.

The new marketing director, Redmond O'Donoghue, like Hayes an ex-Ford man, had to take charge of the group's marketing drive, for Hayes had identified another defect in Waterford's business. It was one, ironically, that had arisen as a direct result of the crystal company's enormous success.

Waterford was the largest producer of quality crystal in the world and Aynsley China had carved out a niche which made it one of the most profitable premium fine bone china manufacturers in the world. But a major problem resided in Waterford's spread of businesses. In June 1986 the position was as follows: the US 49 per cent, Ireland 20 per cent (of which a majority in any case came from sales to American tourists), the UK 12 per cent, Canada 6 per cent, Continental Europe 5 per cent, Australia 2 per cent, the Caribbean and West Indies 4 per cent, and elsewhere 2 per cent.

In reality American sales were a lot higher if sales to American tourists in Europe were also taken into account. In this case total sales to American customers probably amounted to 85 per cent. This factor of course made Waterford highly exposed to the vagaries of the dollar exchange rate.

It became a key plank in the corporate strategy to reduce this exposure and balance it by repeating the success Waterford had had in America with sales to such other major markets as Europe, Japan, Australia and Canada. O'Donoghue's task was to look at Waterford's marketing and see how the company could break into new markets. He redefined Waterford's customer profile and marked out areas that previously had not been developed. In America, for example, Aynsley China was spotted as having greater market potential. A decision was taken to commit more marketing resources to the States and new patterns specifically designed for American tastes were introduced.

Looking more closely at who Waterford's customers were resulted in new designs aimed at the bridal market. The higher margin giftware range was extended and more lighting products, such as chandeliers, lamps and wall brackets, were introduced.

Until Hayes' arrival at Waterford the overseas businesses had been run in a hands-off manner. Hayes and his team set out to tighten the whole system and to introduce specific targets. The manufacturing of the products was no longer to be allowed to dominate but was tuned to market demand. Tighter distribution and inventory control were underpinned by a marketing philosophy based, first and foremost, on what the customer wanted.

A new and major market had been selected as a target – continental Western Europe. This is a market which is often overlooked by Irish and British companies, whose instincts tend to home in on America first. Waterford saw the European market as having great potential. Its total population of 400 million is bigger than the States and in many countries there is a higher disposable income.

Europe represented an obvious alternative, though a hard one, to the problem of too great an American exposure. It was identified by Hayes as a longer term goal. Meanwhile he did not neglect America.

Hayes' overseas strategy exemplifies some of the essentials of his approach. America was undoubtedly a major success for Waterford. By 1986 Waterford had 28 per cent of the crystal stemware market there, 50 per cent of the giftware market and an impressive 92 per cent of the over-$30 stemware business. Just as when he arrived at Waterford, Hayes looked at the whole company and asked a fundamental question: what does it do and why?

So with America. Although successful, Waterford's strategy here was put under the microscope. New products were explored, again with the underpinning of a focused marketing strategy and a drive to integrate manufacturing with demand.

In the summer of 1986 Waterford was able to capitalise on its success in the States. It turned to investors for new funding. In a whirlwind 5-day tour Hayes and his team made a series of highly polished presentations to American financial institutions. They were well received and a successful launch on NASDAQ, the American over-the-counter market, followed. The $42.8m American Depository Receipt (ADR) issue raised valuable new funds. In a stroke Waterford's American profile was raised, it won the support of important American investors and for the first time in nearly two decades debt was eliminated.

The corporate objectives, by now inscribed on the hearts of Waterford executives, were spelt out to the American audience. They were to:

- rationalise the core business

- reduce borrowings

- become more market-driven

- build on their American strengths

- grow in international markets

- motivate employees at all levels

Most important of all, the company declared its intention of increasing the net income by 20 per cent per annum. Before the year was out an opportunity to realise at one stroke many of the company's corporate goals presented itself. It was the acquisition of Wedgwood, one of the most prestigious names in china and a company which before Hayes' arrival and the turnaround of Waterford would have been an unattainable target.

A declared part of Waterford's corporate plan had been to investigate the opportunities for an acquisition in tableware or a related giftware market. 'Wedgwood was obviously a name we had thought of,' says Hayes. 'But when we drew up our 5-year plan, our balance sheet was still too highly geared and we were not then in a position to contemplate such a move.'

Fate was to play its hand. In early 1986 the London International Group made a £149m bid for Wedgwood. Waterford watched helplessly as the bid was rejected by Wedgwood and then was referred to the Monopolies and Mergers Commission. 'We were really worried,' says Hayes. 'There were other bidders on the sidelines and we thought the stake LIG held in Wedgwood might be sold on to a company whose bid would not be referred.'

Wedgwood was clearly a company whose time as an independent

entity was running out. Its end year results showed a profit jump, from £15.1m to £19.5m, but there was a widespread belief that its management had not capitalised on Wedgwood's prestigious name. It was under siege as more bid rumours circulated. There were whispers that major investors in the company were also dissatisfied.

Then Hayes received an important phone call. 'I heard that LIG was losing interest and the 10 per cent stake might be available.'

It was now or never. 'We had suddenly become big enough and fashionable enough to contemplate such a move. It was fortuitous it all came together at the same time,' says Hayes.

Hayes, who claims he did not know the first thing about takeovers and bid manoeuvres, was in the room with two colleagues and one remarked, 'We had better call Warburgs'. Within hours two corporate finance men were in the air to Dublin. The following day Hayes and other directors flew into London. Turning to his colleagues, Hayes remarked, 'We'll not be going home tonight.'

Later that week he phoned Sir Arthur Bryan, Wedgwood's chairman, whose first words were 'I wondered when you'd be calling'. Within 10 days the details of Waterford's offer for Wedgwood were complete and Waterford was ready to ride in as a shining white knight.

The days before the bid became final were both exciting and traumatic. Wedgwood had been relentlessly hostile to LIG but it still did not want to lose its independence. Other companies were suspected of potential interest.

Sir Arthur and his colleagues feared LIG because of its business profile. It had a spread of businesses from condoms to tableware and this was seen as a threat to Wedgwood's high prestige name. In Hayes and Waterford they had a bidder who assured them their name would remain unadulterated. Accordingly they were enthusiastic and friendly.

The deal – fourteen Waterford shares for three Wedgwood shares – valued Wedgwood at £252m. A novel feature incorporated in the package, was that a UK subsidiary, Waterford Wedgwood Holdings, was set up to enable UK holders of Wedgwood shares to receive dividends in sterling and maintain their tax benefits.

On 1 December 1986 Waterford announced it had received acceptances of 87.5 per cent of the issued share capital of Wedgwood.

'We breathed a sigh of relief,' recalls Hayes. 'Someone once said to have a lot of success you also have to have a lot of luck too. I can vouch for that. We took the opportunity when it presented itself but I can say now it will be impossible to get a gem like this again.'

The offer had outstanding commercial benefits, not just for Waterford but for Wedgwood too. The merger combined two of the strongest names and products in the world tabletop industry, with sales of more than £264m in total.

An integrated group can offer significant distribution, marketing and sales efficiencies. Technology and production resources can be shared and distribution and retailing channels combined. Wedgwood had a UK chain of in-store shops which offered Waterford an opportunity to expand UK sales.

At a stroke the deal reduced Waterford's dependence on any one geographic area and offered benefits for Waterford in Europe and Japan, where Wedgwood was stronger. The latter could take advantage of Waterford's strong US presence.

All this did not prevent Paddy Hayes having an even greater attack of nervous anticipation on his first day at Wedgwood. 'It was potentially more traumatic than my first day at Waterford,' he recalls. 'There was a lot to sort out. Although we had some experience in fine china through Aynsley, we were taking on a very complex china business.'

In addition, he was greeted by managers and staff who were uncertain about their future. 'For the first four months I did no paperwork; I just talked to the people there and tried to get to know who the main decision-makers were. I had to understand their strengths and weaknesses. We also had to unravel a very complex business structure. Wedgwood was divided into several business areas.'

But it was a four months he found exhilarating. The task was delicate but, says Hayes, 'We ended up with a first-class management structure. It is highly skilled, highly motivated and highly enthusiastic about the opportunities ahead.'

The boards of the companies were reorganised. The main Waterford board is responsible for overall strategy and a separate company, Waterford Wedgwood Holdings, runs the UK business.

'The main difference in the structure now is that it is more participative and open. It is very discussion-oriented. I think this is suitable in today's conditions. It is certainly suitable for getting the best of the great depth of knowledge and experience at Wedgwood,' says Hayes.

In January 1987 Hayes appointed a new chief executive, Patrick Byrne, at Wedgwood. He sees planning for succession a major leadership task: 'One of my key objectives is to put in a good management development programme to ensure the company is growing a new succession'.

The first thing tackled at Wedgwood was the disposal of several properties and three trading companies which were profitable but were no longer seen as part of the Waterford Wedgwood strategy. 'There was no conflict at all about what should go,' says Hayes.

Waterford expects benefits totalling £18m to flow through to the bottom line in 1988. One-third of this will come from synergistic benefits, £6m from reduced manpower, and a further £6m from the disposal of non-core companies.

'If all goes according to plan we will be well on the road to eliminating borrowing all over again,' says Hayes. Debt rose after the Wedgwood acquisition to around £70m but Hayes vows he will get this down to zero again and repeat the Waterford success.

There are further similarities in Waterford's turnaround strategy for its new acquisition. Stock control again played a central role. Like Waterford, Wedgwood was a manufacturing company which had inventory levels double its sales requirements.

Hayes closed one factory and took a closer look at unprofitable product lines. This meant discontinuing patterns which were not making money. He also stopped the practice of selling distressed merchandise because he argued it damaged Wedgwood's high-class reputation.

Targets for stock control were set at a lower level than Waterford's – not more or less than 5 months' supply of items at any one time. But the same 3 months should be achieved by 1989. In addition, Waterford is looking at the storage of the china products which are the more easily broken or damaged and take up more shelf space. As in America, computer-aided systems have been introduced at major retailers.

In October 1987, Waterford launched its range in Japan. A new stemware pattern, Sovereign, was specially designed for that market. Said Paddy Hayes: 'The Japanese market is notoriously difficult to break into but, building on the outstanding success of Wedgwood, we believe we can develop a valuable business for Waterford in Japan during the next three to five years.'

In Europe too Wedgwood proved to have a small edge on Waterford and Hayes sees the combination of handcrafted crystal goblets and finest china dinner services as unbeatable for the European tabletop. The two companies will make a combined assault on this market.

Waterford's turnaround story is clearly visible in its financial performance. Its year-end 1986 figures, including one month of Wedgwood, show the extent of Hayes' success. While group turnover was reduced because of the disposal of non-core business, pre-tax profits were up 26 per cent to IR£23.3m. Operating margins had doubled from 8.5 per cent to 17.4 per cent.

In the 2 years between 1985 and 1987 Hayes and his team had achieved a profit climb of 37 per cent, an earnings per share increase of 35 per cent and a dividend rise of 44 per cent. Both trading margins and the company's share price had doubled.

The results did, however, reveal a major problem confronting the group. A weak dollar had taken its toll on European tourist buying, and sales weakened in the UK, Ireland and other European markets. This in turn had a knock-on effect on stock levels and of course posed problems with crystal revenue sales in the States. Despite the successful dollar-hedging strategy of Waterford's finance director, Anthony Brophy, Hayes warned the shareholders: 'Should the dollar remain at present levels for any sustained period it will have adverse effects on profits and on volume growth.'

The balancing of US revenue with other markets would clearly take some time, and tackling Europe could take 10 years, but meanwhile a problem had arisen on Hayes' own doorstep in Ireland. It was the high cost base in Waterford's manufacturing operations, which was mainly caused by labour costs in Ireland being double those of workers in American competitor industries.

In July 1987, Hayes was faced with the daunting task of asking for 750 voluntary redundancies from his 3,000 crystal workforce to reduce the company's high costs. The redundancies were part of a three-part plan to restore competitiveness. The plan also included capital investment of IR£18m, increased marketing worldwide and revised work practices.

Having performed the turnaround once, it became obvious that Paddy Hayes had to do it again. Undoubtedly his experience at Ford has armed him with the determination and experience to tackle this problem. There is an apocryphal story about Hayes. In 1984 he walked into the Ford assembly plant canteen and explained to the 800 workers they had just lost their jobs. At the end of his speech they broke into applause.

Hayes is well aware of his reputation as being tough but fair. He sees it as a reflection on his status as a manager of a manufacturing company: 'There are many things that become fashionable in business – computers, finance, marketing. Manufacturing is never fashionable. I'm one of the few executives who has actually got his hands dirty.'

He is relentlessly optimistic. As long as Waterford can tackle the cost base problem to alleviate the pressures of the weak dollar, the future he sees is alluring. He predicts a rising trend of profitability in the order of 8 per cent to 10 per cent a year.

He is clear what will happen then: 'An acquisition. Where and when I do not know now. It could be in Europe, it could be in America, it could be in Britain. It just depends on what comes up.'

This is a comment which has a certain irony on the lips of Paddy Hayes. Companies that need to be turned around are often not in a position to take advantage of what comes up. In Waterford's case they were lucky it happened to be Paddy Hayes.

Waterford agreed subsequently to a management buy-out of Aynsley China for £17.5m. The buy-out enabled the Waterford Glass Group to concentrate its resources on its two world brands, Waterford crystal and Wedgwood Group products. Waterford will use the proceeds to reduce its borrowings and to strengthen its balance sheet.

```
┌─────────────────────────┐
│  3   Low                │
│      & Bonar            │
└─────────────────────────┘
```

by Rebecca Nelson

As recently as 1983 the Dundee-based company Low & Bonar, whose name has long been synonymous with Africa and jute, was experiencing severe difficulties. While this was due in part to the economic climate of the time, it was also the result of the company's having over-diversified and moved into 'oddball' areas, as their chief executive officer, Roland Jarvis, describes them.

Low & Bonar began as a family-owned jute business in Dundee 75 years ago. In the 1940s it went public and by the early 1970s it had gradually introduced outside management as the immediate family played a smaller part. By this time the company had moved into areas such as engineering and even the travel business, but with little success. In 1982 profits had slumped to £3.5m, mainly in the form of unremittable African earnings, and the annual turnover was £174m.

Action had to be taken – and fast.

The board, chaired by Sir Dermot de Trafford, decided to seek a new direction and started to eradicate the under-performing businesses. To take charge of this turnaround venture of self-survival, they headhunted Roland Jarvis from TI Raleigh. From the moment he was appointed in 1984 Jarvis expressed firm ideas on what a chief executive should do – determine the strategy, see that the systems and management are in place to implement it, take important decisions and ensure that the company has a high enough profile in the City. It was with this level of determination that Jarvis achieved the turnaround of Low & Bonar, so that it is now one of Scotland's most successful industrial groups.

The first action Jarvis took following his appointment at Low & Bonar was to embark upon a 6-month programme to learn about the firm's existing businesses, which, outside the UK, were stretched across the former British Empire as far as Africa, Australia, Canada and the Far

East. As a result of this programme, it became clear to Jarvis that the company should abandon its diversification strategy and should aim instead to become a specialised manufacturer of materials and products in four precisely defined markets within the UK, Europe and North America. These were packaging (producing plastic shrink and stretch wrap film, printed plastic bags and cartons), plastics (special containers for materials handling and manufacturers of final products), textiles (producing Flotex floorcovering, polypropylene yarns for such uses as carpets and artificial grass surfaces, and non-woven textiles), and lastly electronics (specialising in power supply and control equipment).

The rationale, which was accepted by the board, was that these core areas had leading-edge technologies, were capable of being niche-market leaders, had good margins and the potential for rapid growth. Any activity that appeared superfluous to these chosen markets was sold off, even when a business had been profitable – a daring but necessary action. These non-core businesses accounted for some £15m–£20m of capital employed, about a third of the total, and the divestment process realised £13m in 1985 and further significant sums thereafter. Businesses disposed of included Bonar Long (heavy transformers), Langley Alloys (specialised castings), and Bonar Stanger, Australia (electrical components).

Simultaneously a considerable reinvestment programme was undertaken, or, as Jarvis puts it, his next task was to 'unlock the cash box'. The bulk of this investment went into the plastic packaging division, which demanded high reinvestment to keep pace with the latest technological development. Now all divisions have substantial investment programmes.

In 1985 there was £10m–£11m of new capital investment, in 1986 £17m and by 1987 £22m. During this period, the textile division invested £10m–£12m in specialised, non-woven textiles, an area Jarvis views as particularly exciting because it is a premium, niche-market product sold at the top end of the market.

In a fifty-fifty joint venture with Eastman Kodak of the USA, Low & Bonar set up a manufacturing company in South Carolina to produce non-woven textiles. Low & Bonar is now sole owner. It also has a new Dundee plant for the production of non-wovens, which will ultimately achieve four times its current capacity, and high-volume production is scheduled to begin very soon.

An examination of the structure of the business shows that it is split between packaging, which accounts for 54 per cent of turnover and 61 per cent of profits, and the other three areas. As Jarvis explains, 'Packaging is a sound stable business but very capital-hungry. It needs to be balanced.' The other three areas are more dynamic in growth terms but less 'capital-hungry', and they have a higher profit-margin potential.

Part of the turnaround strategy included achieving a geographical balance across the spectrum of the four industries – packaging, plastics, textiles and electronics. The target was to have 60 per cent of sales in the UK and Europe and the remainder in the USA and Canada.

When considering a suitable acquisition target, Jarvis and his team discuss the options with their merchant bankers, who in turn run their own assessment of the target. Then a definitive document, which Jarvis relies on during his negotiations, is drawn up and the first contact is made. Such careful planning results in successful acquisitions and mergers.

In March 1987 Low & Bonar completed its acquisition of the French company Flotex SA, and now the two companies plan to take the entire European market by storm. Flotex is marketed as an 'indestructible' electrostatically flocked floor covering for use in hospitals, hotels, offices and domestic kitchens and bathrooms. In 1986 it was launched in Japan and the USA, and currently shows a 40 per cent return on capital. In Jarvis's words, it makes 'superb profits', and is just one of a series of acquisitions made as part of his turnaround strategy.

USI Film, a Texas-based company specialising in low-density film, was acquired for £6.5m cash, thereby strengthening the North American packaging division. Similarly Low & Bonar's electronics interests were developed when two British companies and one American, Powertec, a manufacturer of power supply equipment, were acquired, largely by means of a £22.6m rights issue.

Meanwhile an initial 50 per cent stake in the German company Rhein-Conti had given Low & Bonar an opportunity to introduce Europe to its rotational moulding techniques. According to Jarvis, Low & Bonar is now a world leader in this technology. It has since acquired the balance of the equity in Rhein-Conti and enlarged its European presence by acquiring Fusion Kunststoffen in Holland.

Jarvis stresses that his objective is always to reach a fair and acceptable deal, with the emphasis recently on performance-related buyouts, under which a down payment is made, usually for half the target's equity, and the rest of the sum, which is based on attained profits, paid over the ensuing 2 years.

Jarvis' credo is to have a coherent strategy. He is interested in acquiring companies with good management. After all, what is the point of inheriting problem companies? Low & Bonar's involvement since 1984 and the successful implementation of Jarvis's turnaround strategy have put the company in the enviable position of possessing a vast database on companies that might be of interest.

Today Low & Bonar has a simple, decentralised management structure. The European and North American divisions have their own chief executives, who report directly to Jarvis as managing director and group chief executive. In turn Jarvis controls a close-knit headquarters staff of twenty, whose main duties are to monitor the performance of the divisions and their subsidiaries, set targets and seek out potential acquisitions.

No less an achievement has been Jarvis's communication of the turnaround strategy to his divisional chiefs. Some had come from small private companies or were divisional heads within larger companies. When asked by Jarvis to present him with strategic growth plans for their division, they all did so – enthusiastically.

One of Jarvis's early tasks was to recruit three young, science-based MBAs who were to become a corporate strategy, planning and development team. Through computer databanks and other sources of international information they built up a detailed store of knowledge about Low & Bonar's industries, which in turn enabled them to identify potential opportunities for acquisitions, joint ventures and licensing deals.

If a company is in the throes of being financially turned around, it is necessary that its public profile should be raised, and with it, its sagging share price, which at the end of March 1984 was languishing at around 60 pence with a P/E ratio of 4 for Low & Bonar. To this end Jarvis introduced a financial PR consultancy to promote Low & Bonar to the media, stockbrokers, and the merchant banking fraternity to spread the word that this Dundee company was alert and aggressive, and wanted to know of any opportunities in its main markets.

The results have been considerable. Prior to the October 1987 Stock Market 'crash' the share price hovered around 300p, a P/E ratio of 15.

In 1986 some £17m was invested in existing operations, bringing Low & Bonar's total expenditure on expansion to £100m. In 1987 the total reduced to about £30m, despite several acquisitions. The financial results for the near future are likely to be increasingly impressive. Analysts forecast a pre-tax profits boost to over £20m on a turnover breaking the £300m mark. Jarvis himself forecasts that by 1989 the turnover could be in the region of £500m.

In 3 short years Low & Bonar has transformed itself from an ageing, ailing organisation into a company that can continue in style, safe in the knowledge that it is currently growing at a faster rate than those successful predators Hanson Trust and BTR, that it leads the world in the technology of rotational moulded plastic products, and that it dominates the North American polythene packaging market and makes the world's most indestructible carpet.

Not bad for a 75-year-old Dundee business!

4 Vickers

by Sir David Plastow,
Chairman and Chief Executive, VICKERS PLC

When Vickers and Rolls-Royce Motors merged in 1980, Kenneth Fleet, the much respected financial journalist and former city editor of *The Times*, described the merger as being 'like two drunken earls falling out of Annabel's, leaning against each other for support'. This memorable expression was not one to encourage a new chief executive perhaps, but like many memorable expressions it was also not entirely accurate.

Vickers, a large and 'aristocratic' engineering company, had indeed been staggering about, battered by nationalisation, for a number of years and was clearly in need of a change in direction. On the other hand, Rolls-Royce Motors was a company that had been floated off very successfully when its aerospace parent company had been bankrupted. However, it did seem sensible for Rolls-Royce Motors to be part of a bigger organisation that could help provide the cyclical investment needed to produce new models. The logic of the merger seemed clear to those running both companies, even if it did not to Kenneth Fleet.

My personal experience at Rolls-Royce Motors was to turn out to be a great help to me at Vickers. I had lived through the collapse of the Rolls-Royce parent company in 1971, and seen the effect it had had on the workforce of the car company, which, although unprofitable, had the potential for success. I knew we had to detach ourselves from history and launch ourselves anew at Vickers, in the same way that Rolls-Royce Motors had been floated off separately.

HISTORY

When Vickers began to experience major problems in the late 1960s, it was to some extent the victim of its own proud history. The name of Vickers first appeared in the title of the steel company over 150 years ago, and for over a century Vickers was armourer to the British nation, not to mention half the other nations of the world.

The company's innovation in weaponry is a legend. It produced the first effective machine gun and the first effective tank. It transformed the ironclad battleship into the modern fighting cruiser. Through two world wars and many minor skirmishes the company was at the forefront of the nation, dedicating its engineering initiative almost exclusively to the winning of major conflicts. In time of peace Vickers continued to support defence requirements, but the inevitable post-war slump in demand was always disruptive to the long-term health of the company.

Many attempts were made to widen the manufacturing base, with products ranging from sewing machines to tractors, but success was limited. Governments in the meantime were either unhelpful or positively disruptive. Successive nationalisation of parts of Vickers not only damaged the company directly but made it impossible for the management to pursue a coherent strategy.

Steel was nationalised in 1948 and sold back to the company 6 years later, only to be renationalised in 1967. Unable to pursue a steady course, the company began to suffer. In 1970 four of Vickers' major institutional shareholders, worried about the company's prospects, approached its chairman and asked for a change in top management.

Finally, in 1977, the government perpetrated its final destructive snatch and nationalised the shipbuilding and aircraft businesses painstakingly built up by Vickers. These supplied half the company's sales and two-thirds of its profit. The compensation paid could only be described as grossly inadequate.

1980

The members of the new management team at Millbank Tower in 1980 found that they had inherited an enormously impressive history and were custodians of two of the great names in world engineering. It soon became clear that this history was not a strong foundation on which to build, but more like the burden that Christian in *Pilgrim's Progress* was destined to carry around whilst seeking the promised land.

Despite historical problems it was also clear that the newly merged company had immense potential. In management terms it needed not so much to turn around but to stop trying to go in all directions at the same time. It needed a strategy.

I gave the job of deciding the new management structure to two senior executives – one from Vickers and one from Rolls-Royce – and to referee the debate we brought in an outside consultant. They were all closeted on the 29th floor of Millbank Tower in a room that soon began to resemble a war operations centre, covered in maps and charts, as they took the whole structure of the two companies apart and stuck them back together again. The structure that emerged was simple and effective. Radical surgery was now required.

I have observed a number of unsuccessful amalgamations during my career. I was determined that Vickers and Rolls-Royce should be one homogeneous company and that there would be no fighting factions.

COMMUNICATION

Many changes needed to be made but our first priority was to put a communications system in place. This was to prove vital in enabling us to explain to everyone who worked in the new company precisely what we were doing. As and when difficult decisions were made, we had to make sure that all employees not only knew what we were doing but why we were doing it.

That communications system, which comprised face-to-face briefing cascading down from board level down to the shopfloor, is still in place today. This team briefing was introduced with the help and guidance of The Industrial Society. I insisted it should be installed in every part of the organisation and would allow no exceptions. I made clear to all managers running businesses the dire consequences of failing to establish team briefing.

As the deadline approached, The Industrial Society gave me an update on how installation was progressing. They told me everything was fine – apart from one problem area. I demanded to know who the culprit was – I would soon get him in line – but the answer left me rather red-faced. I was the culprit, having done nothing about installing team briefing at Head Office. This was at the end of November, and I am pleased to say we had fallen in line before Christmas.

Team briefing is now part of our culture. It has enabled us to make radical changes to the company's structure, such as a substantial reduction of the workforce and more competitive approaches to business, and yet still take our employees with us because they understand and agree our long-term aims to become properly effective by international standards.

I firmly believe in 'walking the job'. There is no substitute for going round factories and offices, talking to people about their work and their view of the company. It is also the best way to find out if the team-briefing process is working properly. When I was visiting a factory in the North-East, I asked one of the men on the shopfloor if he knew how the sales and order book of his business were going – basic information that a team briefing should communicate to him. He instantly gave me correct answers and assured me he had recently had an excellent team briefing.

I also asked about the particular job he was working on, and for which customer it was intended. At once he set off and returned with some paperwork which I took to be the job sheet for the order he was working on. However, when he showed it to me, it turned out to be the detailed briefing provided by the managers of that particular site. It had clearly been supplied with the exhortation to all employees to 'for heaven's sake remember the figures because he's bound to ask you these questions!'

This may not have been quite how we saw the information being dispersed but it was certainly effective.

STRATEGY

The new executives next sat down together and developed a strategy to take the business through to a stronger and successful future. The businesses within Vickers were many and varied. We had to decide which were our strengths and which our weaknesses. Having looked long and hard at each and every area, we were able to identify the basic requirements for the businesses that we would retain.

We had four strategic criteria: (1) the business should be a world player, (2) it should be relevant to management skills, (3) it should be in a market with significant growth, and (4) it should have a significant market share.

By world player we meant that the company should be demonstrably internationally competitive and have at least two major markets outside the UK, including the major areas that power the world economy – the USA, Europe and the Far East. The business also had to be relevant to our existing management skills. The new team had reasonably wide experience and a solid management record but we did not want to get outside our area of competence.

We also only wished to run businesses that were selling in a growth market. Some people have made a great success squeezing the best out of sunset industries but we were only interested in developing the company into a long-term success in industries that were still expanding.

Finally, we wanted to be large enough within any particular market to be able to have an effect on that market. We knew that to be able to trade successfully in competitive world markets we had to be a big player even if it was only in a relatively small niche.

DIVESTMENT

Comparing the existing portfolio of companies to our set of criteria was a long and difficult task. What came out of it was a list of businesses which did not fit or clearly could not produce the required profit growth. It must be stressed that previous earnings performance was not the main factor. Some businesses we felt could be developed either by acquiring businesses to put alongside them or investing resources in them to develop products or markets.

It was not a particularly enjoyable period. We had to say goodbye to some twenty companies that had been part of Vickers and Rolls-Royce

Motors for many years. Senior executives were already under a lot of pressure, made much worse by the personal stress of having to implement unwelcome decisions and to dispense with loyal friends and colleagues.

In addition to putting the company into a manageable shape, divestment also brought in money. It was money we badly needed to reduce our borrowings and to provide the cash headroom we needed to develop new products and new manufacturing facilities in the core businesses that were to remain.

One of the first things we discovered was that the gap between a decision and successful implementation can be longer than anticipated when divestment is the object. Perhaps out of naivety, we expected other companies to realise the benefits of acquiring our unwanted companies in order to add to their strength. It took a lot of work but they eventually did.

A good example of successful divestment was the Rolls-Royce Motors Diesel Engine Division, which made a range of diesels for both military and civil applications at very competitive prices. It was just the wrong size to have any serious presence in the world market. Massey Ferguson, however, in the shape of its Perkins Engines Division, was unable to complete its plan for world market coverage as it did not have the full range of horsepowers. The missing part coincided neatly with the Rolls-Royce range.

It was therefore quite logical to sell the diesel business to Perkins in a deal satisfactory to both parties. I had worked with Rolls-Royce Diesels since my early days in Rolls-Royce Motors; and to see the company sold to a new parent, who not only gave it a good home but was able to develop it better than we could, seemed to me at the time to represent a turning point.

The sale of Vickers Australia – a 66-per-cent-owned subsidiary mainly involved in heavy engineering – illustrates the importance of divesting in a careful and sensible manner. The Australian company was in an industry sector which was clearly outside our strategic criteria. It included foundries, dockyards and mining equipment, but the over-capacity in heavy engineering in Australia did not make the business attractive to buyers.

Careful negotiation helped find a solution. BHP of Australia also had a large heavy-engineering company, Commonwealth Steel, which needed to be rationalised. So in 1983 we formed Comsteel Vickers, a company in which we and BHP owned 38 per cent. The new company was better able to compete during difficult times and eventually, at the very end of 1985, we were both bought out entirely by ANI, a large Australian engineering company. This two-step process had succeeded where divestment looked almost impossible, and enabled us eventually to sell out at a reasonable price. The disposal of our final stake in Comsteel Vickers was also our final move out of heavy engineering. In many ways it seemed like the shedding of the final part of that burden of history we inherited in 1980.

We also divested ourselves of a sizeable property portfolio. As an engineering company, we should produce for our investors a return on capital employed of 20 per cent or more. But our property interests, which were quite considerable, were delivering something in the region of 6 per cent. The decision to dispose of them was not difficult, and finding a home for them was somewhat easier than with some of our manufacturing divestments.

ACQUISITIONS

Divestments brought down our gearing fairly rapidly, and even before the company was showing signs of substantial revival, we were on the lookout for acquisitions. Once again we found a gap between decision-making and being able to put that decision into practice, but eventually we started acquiring relatively modest companies that would strengthen those businesses we were determined to keep and expand. However, making acquisitions could not really start until we had a track record that convinced the City we were through the worst of our troubles and could be relied on to make the right choices.

The history of Vickers is scattered with false starts and the company had the reputation of being accident-prone. This reputation was sustained in 1983 when poor results at Rolls-Royce reversed the upward trend in profits.

However, we did learn from the start that being very open with the City is the best way to keep it on our side. We never tried to hide our problems and spent a great deal of time and effort in communication with our shareholders and bankers.

RESEARCH AND DEVELOPMENT

When a company is being restructured and rebuilt, there is always a lot of talk of financial stringency and a tight hold on the purse strings, but I think it is essential that this should not be to the detriment of necessary investment in improved manufacturing facilities and research and development. In particular it is very easy to dispense with long-term research and development to bolster short-term financial success. However, the future of British engineering companies rests on their ability to produce unique products which can claim a niche in world markets by their superiority.

We were careful therefore during the difficult period in the early 1980s to maintain our spending on R&D – over £21m in 1981 and £25m in 1982. But we ensured that this was spent in areas where we could see ourselves exploiting that crucial market niche.

MANAGEMENT STRUCTURE

Above all, I knew we had to change the management culture of Vickers. Some parts of the company appeared to have been preserved in aspic. New management systems and planning processes would be needed to do this, but in one simple way we demonstrated the new approach to everyone in the company. We abandoned the separate dining facilities, we swept away the director's suites and managers' luncheon rooms and replaced them in all our factories, and our Head Office, with single status dining. This is not merely an egalitarian idea; it lets the workforce know that we want its co-operation, and are aware of its importance in the success of the corporation. I am sure there is no better way of convincing the established manager that things are changing than by suddenly transforming the style in which he takes his lunch!

Although the importance of good management cannot be over-estimated, it is also vital to get the management structure of a company sorted out, particularly when that company is undergoing wholesale changes. Between 1980 and 1984 Vickers had a main board which included five group chief executives familiarly known as 'Feudal Barons'. These directors each controlled a fiefdom of companies and reported through the Managing Directors Committee. It put a man in charge of a business who understood the business under his control, and it worked during the years of restructuring and divestment. However, it created a rather long line of reporting from the people at the sharp end of the businesses to the Chief Executive.

Having reduced the number of principal operating companies within Vickers by divestment and rationalisation from over fifty in 1980 to under twenty by the end of 1984, we were in a position to reflect this reduction at Head Office by simplifying our own management structure. If you require people in the businesses to retrench and to use their resources more effectively, you must also reflect this action at corporate headquarters. Head Office costs were sharply reduced in line with the reduction demanded of individual businesses.

So in 1984 one layer of management at main board level – the 'Feudal Barons' referred to earlier – was removed. These chief executives of main business groups with their own head-office structure represented a degree of over-organisation and were no longer needed. The number of businesses within the group had been reduced and the remaining portfolio had been gathered together into logical and coherent groups. It was felt that two deputy managing directors could handle these groups between them.

The resulting executive committee, which still operates today, consists of a Chairman and Chief Executive, the Managing Directors, the Commercial Director, the Development Director, the Finance Director and the Director of Public Affairs. Ever since this committee was first set up, it has met every Monday and, given the short lines of communication, is able to make a speedy response to requests from the businesses whilst also tackling broader corporate decisions.

The committee is only able to do its job properly because of the management systems imposed on Vickers soon after the new management took over in 1980. Accurate management information is essential to all decision-making.

FINANCIAL REPORTING

Knowing the up-to-date and exact financial situation of the company, obviously vital in the difficult days of 1980, is equally vital in the stronger situation of 1988. The problem I perceived on my arrival was that there was considerable delay in results from the businesses reaching group headquarters. It could take up to 6 weeks to get month-end results, and this was clearly unacceptable.

The Finance Director immediately instituted a system of reporting which ensured that we got a first flash report of the month's figures from each and every business 3½ days after the end of the period. I am sure that at the time this speed of reporting was unique for a British multi-business, worldwide manufacturing company. Even today this is an impressive system that few can beat. Full figures are available within 2 weeks of the flash reports, and invariably these are within 1 and 2 percentage points of the first report.

This up-to-date financial information is critical to a company that is undergoing major surgery. When cash is short, it is important to know if you are bleeding to death from one of your limbs sooner rather than later; and when recovery starts, it is vital to be constantly aware how a business's figures relate to its budget. It is all very well to have faith that your strategy criteria have sorted out the businesses that will be successful but, as not every decision is 100 per cent correct, monitoring of progress is still needed to help you sleep at night.

PLANNING PROCESS

We had a corporate strategy but we also knew that each business within the group needed its own strategy and business planning. A new planning process introduced into Vickers at the beginning of 1981 is the key to the controlled direction and knowledge the centre must have to guide and help its businesses and to aid the general strategy.

The Vickers planning process consists of three separate stages. We start in early spring with a strategic document, which leads to a business plan in early summer and an operating plan by November. At each stage the business presents its case to the centre for discussion. Once the strategy is agreed, the business produces its plan for the next 3 years, based on that strategy. This too is discussed and refined for input from the centre. Finally, the detailed operating plan for the next year is agreed.

From the start we found that these set disciplines for planning were essential, but we always tried to keep the style informal, allowing wide discussions before detailed targets were set. Although all successful companies have a disciplined planning process, we like to think that it is the very openness of our approach that enables us at the centre to come up with the best planning decisions.

Not only does this process provide control from the centre but it also ensures that we know enough about the activities of each business and their long-term thinking to enable us to contribute where appropriate. Help and not interference is our motto.

MANAGEMENT INCENTIVES

One of the greatest problems for a struggling company is low morale and lack of commitment in senior management. When I first joined Vickers in 1980, it became clear that not only did we have to give our managers room to manage but that it was incumbent upon us to offer them the incentive to make a success of their businesses. They had previously observed the company teetering close to the brink of disaster, and many must have been considering whether this was the time to leave.

We therefore introduced a scheme for senior management based upon return on capital employed. Targets are set at the operating plan stage. It is possible for management to make 25 per cent bonuses on already high salaries if they reach their targets. They drop 5 per cent for every 1 per cent fall but gain 3 per cent for 1 per cent improvement.

There are no exceptions or excuses. Should a supplier strike prevent Rolls-Royce Motor Cars reaching its target, bonuses would not be paid. If Howson-Algraphy, our printing-plate manufacturer in Leeds, were to have a disastrous fire, then their bonuses would also go up in smoke – unless of course they had sophisticated contingency plans to overcome the problems fast.

The maximum payment is a 60 per cent addition to basic salary and this scheme is available to the directors of all our businesses. These incentive payments have already motivated our management and have produced a very high standard through the company.

However, inevitably, there have been considerable management changes. Between 1980 and 1985 over 60 per cent of the top 300 managers in Vickers changed, but the most revealing statistic is that only 25 per cent of the new appointments came from outside the company. Unleashing this considerable talent from within the company is now paying handsome dividends.

CORPORATE IDENTITY

It was important to demonstrate to the public at large that Vickers was a new and different company, so we did the obvious thing and changed our corporate identity. The Vickers feathers – so much associated with the old days of Vickers, the armaments supplier – were abolished in favour of a modern, clear-lined logo suggesting the technological and precision engineering that the new Vickers wished to be known for. I think it is a tribute to our success in communicating the real structural changes in the company that the new identity became accepted very quickly outside the company and, perhaps even more importantly, within.

We also did something rather unusual to change our image. At a time when we were still divesting and selling companies, we bought a company plane. Many people regard the buying of a twin-engined jet as the last folly of a chief executive. However, it was not the chief executive that bought the jet, it was the company. From the moment we first got it, it was put to work taking the customers of all of our businesses to destinations right across Europe to show them our products. We knew that all our companies had to get out and sell their wares, and not only in the UK, and the jet – complete with the Vickers livery – represented the new forward looking side of Vickers. It showed that we were not shrinking the company down to almost nothing, but preparing to move ahead – fast!

The plane certainly earned its keep, working just as much for the smallest companies as it did for Rolls-Royce Motor Cars and I am happy to say that we have now replaced it with a new and slightly larger jet. Incidentally, less than 5 per cent of the aircraft's flying time is taken up transporting members of the board.

THE BOTTOM LINE

In the final analysis it is by its results that a company is judged, and perhaps the best pointer to a company's success is earnings per share. In 1982, when the new-style Vickers was beginning to emerge, earnings per share were standing at 14p, but by 1986 earnings had risen to 40.7p. Perhaps an even more dramatic turnaround is demonstrated by the figures for profit per employee. In 1982 this stood at £750 per employee, but in 1986 the figure was £3,400.

During the same period we also balanced the geographical spread of the markets for our products. For many years the curse of British engineering companies was over-reliance on the home market and the Commonwealth. We set all our businesses the task of seeking out a market share in the major economies of the world: 26 per cent of the sales are now in the world's biggest economy, the United States, and we are capturing a growing share in the Far East.

CONCLUSION

In 1980 there were over fifty separate operating businesses in the portfolio. In 1987, when we were already into our acquisition phase, there were only twenty, and these businesses, with a couple of small exceptions, fit into our six key business areas: Rolls-Royce Motor Cars, lithographic plates, business furniture, defence and aerospace, medical and scientific equipment, and marine engineering.

We still run our strategy criteria over these companies as we did in the early days. We still check that they are internationally competitive and sizeable players in their particular niche. We are now beginning to add to them, to strengthen their position and to ensure that the growth of the company continues at a reasonable rate, even though the turnaround has been achieved.

When I read through this chapter on Vickers since 1980, it all seems rather easy and obvious. We tend to forget the more difficult moments. For example, up to and until 1986 we had to put up with the uncertainty about whether we were going to get adequate compensation for the 1977 nationalisation. This had a destabilising effect on the share price, and in the end we received no extra money, for the European Court of Human Rights rejected our final plea.

It would have been very easy to have been distracted from our plans by those who saw the government policy of privatisation as an ideal opportunity for us to get back into the areas which had been so savagely snatched from us. This would have been a major error. We had found a new and dramatic direction for the company, and any attempt to go back would only have brought back the shadow of 'the bad old days'.

I shall always be grateful to the Company Secretary, in the early 1980s, when we were being pressurised to get back into the old nationalised areas. He came to me to discuss this very problem, and although his whole life had been bound up with Vickers' great triumphs in shipbuilding and aircraft, and he was the archivist of the company, he declared his full agreement and support for the new path upon which the company was set.

We have had of course some hiccups along the way. I probably made a mistake by making too many bullish predictions – perhaps in the interest of bolstering the morale of my colleagues and myself – which we were not able to meet within our original timetable. We now prefer to get on and do things, and point out to people how successful we have been when we have the figures to show it.

The amount of work undertaken by the senior management to turn Vickers round was nothing short of Herculean. However, I am not one of those who believes that the management should work 25-hour days all the time. When the company was in the doldrums it was necessary, but at other times it is crucial to keep a little management energy in reserve, so that if something serious occurs, the extra resource is there.

Some of the more difficult times were not much fun. Hard and painful decisions had to be made and carried out, and we could not possibly enjoy some of these. But I must stress that my philosophy is to enjoy the life of the company. It was a privilege to take on the task of amalgamating and redeveloping two great names of British engineering. The new Vickers is now on a firm and upward course. I am not going to make any dramatic predictions, however, as the management of growth is, if anything, more difficult than the organisation of a turnaround.

Much is yet to be done. But both within the company and in the country as a whole we have the environment that gives us every chance of success.

5 Kwik-Fit

For cynical journalism it's hard to beat financial commentators when a former darling of the stock market takes a severe downturn on its annual results. That's when the cliché merchants move in with their headlines, and nowhere more so than in the automotive components sector. 'Tired and exhausted' ran the *Investors Chronicle* leader, 'Deflated' said the *Guardian*, when Kwik-Fit's downturn in profits was revealed in the figures published after the financial year end in February 1982. Shares dropped to 50p, and later reached a low of 26p. Five years later the *Guardian* commented that Kwik-Fit 'Bolts together another record', while the *Financial Times* went the whole hog with 'Kwik-Fit has disengaged the handbrake, revved up the engine and pressed the accelerator'. With scrip issues of one for ten in April 1983 and one for four in November 1986, the share price reached 226p on 1 July 1987 – equivalent, allowing for the bonuses, to 310p, a twelvefold increase within 5 years.

Tom Farmer, the youngest of seven children, was brought up in Leith in Edinburgh. He left school at 14 to work for Tyreservices Great Britain as a trainee salesman. He left in 1964 to start his own tyre shop, Tyre and Accessory Supplies, in Buccleuch Street, Edinburgh, which he rented for £5 per week. With the abolition of retail price maintenance, business boomed and he soon had three employees. By 1968, when Tyre Accessory Supplies had expanded to five depots, with a turnover of £400,000 and profits of £40,000, it was bought for £400,000 by Albany Tyre Services. Farmer, aged 27, joined the Board of Albany with specific responsibility for expansion north of Birmingham. In 1970 Albany merged with Brown Brothers, and after several disagreements over management philosophy, Tom Farmer left the company and 'retired' to San Francisco. Whilst there he was very impressed with the growth of 'muffler' shops, so impressed in fact that he came out of 'retirement', returned to Britain, acquired two properties in Edinburgh and opened the first Kwik-Fit depot at McDonald Road in 1971. Farmer was then 30 years old.

By 1973 there were ten centres trading, with a turnover of £436,000 and profits of £48,000. Kwik-Fit was then acquired by G. A. Robinson, a mini-conglomerate based in Wolverhampton, for a sum of £700,000. Tom Farmer, a major shareholder in the company, was appointed to the Board. In 1975, after the collapse of the property market and the 3-day working week, the majority of Robinson's businesses were making losses. Tom Farmer acquired the shareholdings of the other directors, took control of the company, sold off everything except the fast-fit operation, and changed the company's name back to Kwik-Fit.

Expansion in depots resulted in annually increasing turnover and profits, and Kwik-Fit became a growth stock. For the financial year ending 28 February 1978 Kwik-Fit had grown to forty-five outlets and showed a turnover of £9.8m and £0.8m profits; 1979 produced figures of £11.5m and £1.15m respectively, and 1980 £15.8m and £1.96m. The trend accelerated in 1981, when turnover reached £29.3m and profit £4.01m. Then in 1982 Farmer reported sales of £34.4m and profits of £1.56m. 'There will be a question mark over Kwik-Fit for a while,' wrote *The Times*. Yet, to a great extent, changes in the organisation and structure of the business in the preceding years which affected these figures were laying the foundations for the company's development since.

Perhaps only John Davis in the *Observer*, who had taken an interest in the development of Kwik-Fit, showed some percipience. 'Kwik-Fit's Tom Farmer has an overall aim – to make his firm the Marks & Spencer of the motorparts trade. He has introduced computerised stock control, improvements in staff communications and staff training and is guaranteeing a good service to customers. It has been expensive . . . but in the long run, it will prove to have been money well spent. Shares have not yet received the message of what is really going on.'

In 1980 Tom Farmer accomplished two successive major acquisitions. The Kwik-Fit chain, now with some fifty-two depots, but mainly in Scotland and the North of England, needed representation in the South if it was to become a national chain. In January 1980, for a £10m purchase, he acquired Euro Exhausts, which owned and managed sixty outlets in the South. Six months later he heard of the appointment of a new chief executive for the Firestone UK operation. A little research showed Farmer that in each of the previous areas in which the CEO had managed, he had disposed of the retail operation. He made contact. 'Are you interested in selling the Firestone depots?' he asked. There was little hesitation – 'Yep' came the answer. 'How much?' asked Farmer. Having arrived with a blank cheque in his pocket, he agreed immediately to the quoted book value of £3.25m. Within days there had been a quick analysis of the 180 depots that had been purchased. Farmer knew a 100 or so quite well, because they had been in his own original chains at Albany & Robinson; the bulk of these and a few of the others were kept, and the remaining eighty were sold to Dunlop, at its request, for £3.25m. So, very suddenly, Kwik-Fit had expanded from fifty depots to over 200.

The Euro takeover was a sizeable meal in itself, and the Firestone depots must have seemed to outsiders like some form of gluttony; in truth, the small management team at Kwik-Fit's head office in Edinburgh was soon suffering from management indigestion. There were now three different managements – the original Kwik-Fit, the old-established Euro, and a group of Firestone depots in varying degrees of furbishment and with marketing areas which in some cases complemented and in others competed with Kwik-Fit's and Euro's. The problem in creating a co-ordinated organisation could well have lasted longer than it did had not Farmer already begun to strengthen his management team.

At the end of 1980 John Padget, a one-time manager at Tenneco, the American oil giant with which Farmer did business, had joined the Board of Kwik-Fit as a non-executive director. Padget was now working in Amsterdam as a business consultant. At about the same time David Jenkins, formerly of Michelin and a business acquaintance of long standing, joined as Sales Director. He was soon touring the country 7 days a week to assess priorities in the welding together of three disparate companies. Thirdly, in October 1980 Farmer had made contact with Harry Shepherd, the head of communications at Marks & Spencer, whose early retirement had been featured in the *Financial Times* and *Management Today*. Farmer had already appreciated that he was in the retail and not the garage business and he retained the services of Shepherd's new marketing and communications consultancy to further his aim of turning Kwik-Fit into the Marks & Spencer of the sector.

Farmer was quite clear on the problems that faced his business in management and personnel, in communications and training and in information gathering. But change was happening already, and the business was due to undergo nothing less than a transmogrification.

With Euro had come an inefficient computerised system, producing statistics after a time-lag that rendered them useless. Kwik-Fit meanwhile was manually logging and checking sales, purchases and stock.

Padget and Farmer were examining information systems to replace these outmoded and inefficient methods. UK software suppliers contacted by Kwik-Fit all shared a common failing: their off-the-peg systems were all they could provide, and they were all unsuitable. Unable to understand retailing, they wanted to cut the customer down to fit their suit.

John Padget and Farmer discussed an article they had read in the *Wall Street Journal* about Church's Fried Chicken, a fast food company with over 1,000 outlets in the US, which had encountered similar difficulties in setting up a computer system tailor-made to their needs, and had finally found salvation with a company called Transaction Control Industries. Don Herlihy, the President of TCI and himself an ex-retailer, was shortly afterwards to be found working in a Kwik-Fit depot, learning the requirements and suggesting the answers.

In March 1982, coinciding with the end of the financial year and just as the financial correspondents were sharpening their pencils and coining the clichés, each of the 200 depots in the Kwik-Fit chain received its terminal and went on-line to two new ICL mainframes at the Edinburgh head office. These point of sale terminals in Kwik-Fit were christened MAT (Management Action Terminals). Herlihy had appreciated the necessity to take into account the attitude of the users of the terminals at the sharp end, including fitters, who had probably never seen, let alone used, a computer terminal, and who all appeared to have very big hands. The terminals had been custom-built to be both effective and easy to operate, and they could even withstand coffee being poured over them. Since Farmer had satisfied himself that his own young son could be quickly trained into an efficient operator, he knew that staff training could overcome all the traditional staff aversions.

MAT was understandably viewed with apprehension by managers and staff in the early training sessions, but almost immediately became an important and valued member of the team. Within days managers were welcoming the elimination of paperwork, with the time saved being used for the customer's benefit. Every night after the close of the day's business the central computers at Edinburgh were calling up each depot on existing telephone lines. Before Tom Farmer even took his shower the following morning, he knew all the details of sales, cash, deliveries, transfers, expenses, banking and price changes, and profits. From being three businesses with three different and inefficient systems, overnight Kwik-Fit had changed into one of the most computerised retailers in the United Kingdom.

Meanwhile, the management team was grappling with the requirements for efficient training, improved communications and how to motivate managers and staff to improve customer service. At Kwik-Fit's first annual conference in June 1981 these ideas were made public to the staff, and in June 1982 Farmer opened the first Kwik-Fit training and development centre.

Sited at Newcastle-under-Lyme, a central location convenient for a national chain, it was purpose-built at a cost of £250,000, and contained a cinema, two classrooms, a reception area with MAT, and a fully equipped and fitted workshop with ramps, hydraulic lifts, tyre racks, exhaust bins, tyre removal and computerised wheel balancing equipment – in other words, all the hardware to be found in a standard Kwik-Fit depot. Kwik-Fit's training programme had begun.

It was also becoming possible to see the company's philosophy now being demonstrated in practice. The philosophy, Farmer has said, was a mix of ingredients. The company was committed to the bulk buying of top-quality components in order to achieve good prices which could then be passed on to customers. Now it was possible to add that the company intended to train to levels previously unknown in the motor industry, to provide competent technical assistance which, together with courteous and efficient service, would get customers back on the road with a minimum of delay.

Kwik-Fit was intending to provide while-you-wait service more cheaply than its competitors. But 1980–1 had not stopped Farmer thinking about the next chain that would develop alongside Kwik-Fit, offering additional but different specialist services. In August 1982 the first Stop'n'Steer depot opened at Piershill in Edinburgh, specialising, as its name implied, in brakes and steering. Farmer's intentions now became clear. Kwik-Fit was a 'bolt off, bolt on' operation based on appointment-free fast service and menu pricing. Now the formula was to be repeated with specialised services. Farmer had chosen the new name 'Stop'n'Steer' in order to position the service as a specialist operation within the car repair market.

But all these different aspects of development were draining expenditure from the Kwik-Fit business. The financial year 1981–2 was a year in which such investment was not to be offset by increased turnover. The economic recession was biting. Fuel had become extremely expensive and the motorist was cutting back. The winter had seen exceptionally bad weather. In the industry overproduction of both tyres and exhausts had led to dumping and corresponding pressure on margins. Farmer mentioned all these reasons when the results were announced, but this hardly assuaged the disappointment of the market.

While these problems were weighing on the sector as a whole, Kwik-Fit was relatively worse off than its competitors because of the expansion programme the company had tackled following the 1980 mergers. The Firestone outlets alone had lost £1.3m in their first year of operation. The market did not just see a deceleration in the company's previous growth, but assumed that the company had gone ex-growth all together.

A great deal of management's attention was still devoted to the problems of administration and motivation. There were a few senior managers who had worked with Farmer in his earliest days when he started on his own account in the tyre business in 1963, and they had followed him devotedly into the new Kwik-Fit. Farmer intuitively appreciated that with good people in the business you could do almost anything, but if the people were not right, even the best ideas would founder.

As early as 1981 his annual report had stated, 'our most important resource is our staff'. In his speech at the opening of the Newcastle-under-Lyme training depot Farmer had said, 'Unfortunately we are in an industry which gives its customers inferior service.' He had gone on, 'I don't believe that people in our industry are bad, but I do accept that they are not always given the right lead by their managers or the right opportunities for training.'

With expansion in mind, it was obvious that Kwik-Fit needed not only to offer a training programme but to create career opportunities that would attract good applicants from fields other than the traditional garage sector. Bringing in new people was obviously not enough; they had to be brainwashed into understanding that the customer was the life-blood of the business and that customer care created the foundations for business growth. 'There is no better advertisement for a company,' Shepherd had said at the Annual Staff Conference, 'than the wagging tongue of the satisfied customer.'

Kwik-Fit's internal communications programme began to operate. The first issue of a weekly *Kwik News* was published in 1982, the earliest symbol of a communications network which was to become so comprehensive that *Management Today* in 1986 would say 'Possibly no workforce in Britain is subject to more sustained corporate hype than Kwik-Fit fitters. Notices emphasising shared commitment are everywhere; they would put a Russian factory to shame . . .'

Farmer had also appreciated that in a sector viewed with suspicion by customers, and perhaps even more particularly by the media and consumer organisations, including Trading Standards Officers, the good and the bad became tarred with the same brush. It was essential that Kwik-Fit's public perception reflected the reality of the newly created company. Hand in hand with the programme of internal communication, therefore, a corporate publicity strategy was developed.

In 1981 Shepherd formed a committee to discuss the problems experienced by motorists with garages. It included consumer experts Baroness Phillips and Jim Humble; car buff Michael Rodd, a TV producer; and Sydney Harris, the 'average' motorist. It was soon obvious that more detail was needed to explain the annual statistics published by the Office of Fair Trading. Although Kwik-Fit could not participate, to ensure objectivity and independence, Farmer agreed to sponsor in-depth research. CARS, the Committee on Automotive Repairs and Servicing, was born.

Research Bureau Limited was commissioned in 1982 to research motorists' perceptions and experience of franchised and independent garages and the fast-fit sector. Reports were published annually in 1983, 1984 and 1985, when Gallup took over, to conduct a much broader study, published in 1986. The initial reports, strongly critical of the way garages approached 'service' – as well as servicing – and charting the rise of the fast-fit sector, were criticised by the motoring organisations. They had no love for Farmer, who had created a very successful business out of operations they had neglected.

Motor Trade Executive, the journal of the Motor Agents Association (MAA), the body which created and enforced the voluntary code of conduct for member garages, was amongst the severest critics of CARS and its surveys. But, as report followed report, the research gradually became accepted as independent, authentic and credible. In 1986 David Gent, Director-General of the MAA, joined the CARS Committee, and the official body of traditional garages now formally co-sponsored the 1987 survey.

Kwik-Fit also began to host a series of seminars organised by ITSA, the Institute of Trading Standards Administration. These seminars provided a forum for representatives of both organisations to exchange information on their common objectives of consumer protection and satisfaction, and were designed to promote greater understanding and co-operation and higher standards within the industry.

Farmer was on record as saying, 'Businesses who take something out of their communities must put something back; it is a moral responsibility but it is also good business.' This doctrine of social responsibility was demonstrated in a number of ways. Kwik-Fit became a regular and large user of the YTS schemes, bringing into the business for training about 140 youngsters annually on 3-month residential courses in conjunction with the Road Transport Industry Training Board. Most of these trainees subsequently joined the business, and some eventually became partners and master managers.

Kwik-Fit became an enthusiastic and committed member of SCOTBIC (Scottish Business in the Community), under the Presidency of the Prince of Wales. Farmer donated £50,000 to sponsor a local enterprise trust created under SCOTBIC, called 'Glasgow Opportunities', and its 'Meet the Buyers' exhibition. SCOTBIC's premier annual award for Business Enterprise for the 3 years 1987–9 is a £5,000 prize donated by Kwik-Fit, and the Scottish Community Education Council's launch of the Young Scot Enterprise package, supported by SCOTBIC, numbers among its backers Tom Farmer and Kwik-Fit.

Inculcating social responsibility within the business was obviously no less important. The Kwik-Fit code of practice had been launched in September 1981 to become the bible of depot behaviour. It is worth reprinting here:

Our code of practice means that the staff of this depot will:

Treat your vehicle with care and fit protective seat covers
Examine your vehicle with you and give an honest appraisal of the work required
Give, on request, a binding quotation before work commences
Ensure that all work is carried out in accordance with the Company's laid down procedures
Inform you immediately of any complications or delays
Examine all finished work with you before your vehicle leaves the premises
Make available to you, on request, all parts removed from your vehicle

We never want our customers to have any doubts about our recommendations

If you have a query, speak to the Manager who is here to help you

As early as 1981 a free share allocation scheme for staff with more than 3 years' service had been launched. In September 1983, at a seminar held by the magazine *Tyres and Batteries*, known throughout the industry as TAB, and chaired by Lord Thorneycroft, Tom Farmer gave a paper on 'Giving the consumer what he wants'. This he knew was impossible unless he had the complete commitment of staff in a sector where caring for the customer tended to be at best spasmodic. Building customer loyalty through service excellence was one side of the coin; appreciating that staff commitment to the company is an important motivation, the other.

In 1984, a master manager and partner scheme was launched in Kwik-Fit, which showed that as a revolutionary thinker in business Farmer was ahead of his sector, if not of his time. Staff who had demonstrated that they had the skills and drive necessary to develop their own and their staff's future were appointed 'master managers', responsible for the running of a centre. They received a share of the centre's profits in addition to their salary. Groups of three centres became the responsibility of a 'Kwik-Fit partner'. As well as being responsible for his own base centre, the partner was responsible for ensuring standards of customer service and profitability at the other two centres in his 'partnership'. The partners' remuneration included a share of the profits from each of the three centres. Two years later, profit sharing was extended to all field staff so that everyone in the centres had a powerful incentive to reduce costs and to maximise both sales and profits.

Small wonder that *Scottish Business Planner* in September 1986 wrote the following. 'Tom Farmer, one of Scotland's best known entrepreneurs, growing from lad o'pairts earning a few shillings of an evening cleaning cookers into a millionaire business tycoon, is one of the most forward thinking managers to come out of Britain since the war.'

In July 1983 Peter Holmes, the former Managing Director of Kwik-Fit's advertising agency, had joined the company as its Marketing Manager. In 1985, Kwik-Fit, working with Hall's Advertising, a part of the Saatchi Group, launched the 'Kwik-Fitter' campaign, whose jingle has already passed into the litany of famous sing-along commercials. But it was more than just a catchy tune; 'You can't get better' became a promise, not just of customer satisfaction, but of staff commitment. Awareness of the Kwik-Fit name among motorists reached 92 per cent in 1986 and business boomed.

Holmes had joined an already established management team in charge of the day-to-day operations of the company. It included Desmond Farmer, Tom's brother, who played a big part in the MAT introduction and subsequently headed systems and personnel. He subsequently left to found his own consultancy. Robert Huthersall, the company secretary, and John Clark, responsible for field sales management, were the other senior executives. And in November 1983 Duncan Whyte, C.A., formerly managing partner of the Group's auditors, Arthur Andersen & Co., in Edinburgh, became Director of Finance to complete the team.

Demonstrating its growing reputation as a retailer offering both services and goods, Kwik-Fit launched its first own-label product under the brand name Centaur. Exhausts, remould tyres, steel radial tyres, batteries, shock-absorbers and radiators followed one another under the Centaur brand name into the chain of rapidly growing Kwik-Fit and Stop'n'Steer outlets, providing an increasing proportion of total sales year by year.

On one of Tom Farmer's early sites, which he owned in the year 1965, sold in 1969, and which came back under the Kwik-Fit banner when the Firestone group was taken over, Farmer opened in 1985 the new Kwik-Fit group headquarters. What to any other business would be a Head Office is to Farmer simply the place where he and the support staff work. The retail outlet is local, and its team of staff work locally to ensure that customers get 100 per cent satisfaction. The Edinburgh operation is there to provide logistical support for that policy.

Adjacent to it, and opened later in 1985, was the company's second training and development centre. The company was now assuming a different dimension. Training courses dealt not only with technical and product knowledge and depot management but sales methods and communication skills. In 1986, to shorten communication lines and improve efficiency still further, Kwik-Fit was formed into five divisions, many of them with divisional directors who had worked with Tom Farmer in his very early days in the tyre business. In 1987, to support the high profile of training and to maintain an objective and professional approach, Kwik-Fit, together with David Jenkins, had formed a separate company which reviewed and revised Kwik-Fit's training programme and became responsible for the training function of the company. Modular training programmes were introduced at the two training and development centres and at the five divisional training offices, as well as in depot training. Sales, technical, administration and management development programmes, supported by sophisticated video and audio-visual material either on their own or as part of an extended course were to ensure instruction and implementation of all of the specialised tasks that were undertaken within the Kwik-Fit operation. As Farmer said in the Kwik-Fit 1987 Report, 'The benefits of investing time, money and energy in training are threefold – first it enables our staff to improve and extend their skills, resulting in a better service to customers. Second, improving customer relations means greater profitability for our business. Third, the group has the right calibre of staff available to achieve our goals.'

The end of the financial year 1987, at the end of a 5-year period from the initial trauma, is perhaps a good vantage point from which to survey how those early developments in the business have worked through (see Figure 5.1). By the end of that period Kwik-Fit was acknowledged as Europe's leading tyre and exhaust retailer. Sales had exceeded £100m in the year for the first time, and profits of £11.1m, representing a 10.82 per cent return on sales, were up 67.5 per cent from the 1986 profits. A report in *The Times* business section said that the 'Strong growth arose principally from three factors'.

The first factor was the continued development in the number of outlets. In the year under review Kwik-Fit had opened twenty-one new outlets and extensively refurbished fourteen more. At the end of February 1982 there were some 223 outlets, including twenty in Europe. The Annual Report and Accounts dated 28 February 1987 showed that the total had become 343, including forty-one in The Netherlands and Belgium. By June 1987 that had become 353, with another forty under development in the UK. Many of these outlets bore little resemblance to those that Farmer and his small team were operating at the beginning of the decade, for in 1986 Kwik-Fit had opened the first of a string of large auto centres which combined under one roof both Kwik-Fit and Stop'n'Steer outlets and a vastly increased range of goods and services. All at fixed prices, these included total car servicing, clutch replacements, brake and steering parts repair and replacement, engine oil and filter change services, suspension repairs, wheel alignment and steering geometry checks and adjustments. Some of these services were being extended during the year to some of the larger Kwik-Fit depots themselves.

The strategy of planned growth in both the number of depots and, secondly, the range of goods and services, reaped its reward, attracting nearly 3 million customers by February 1987. To these individual motorists had been added a whole raft of fleet customers. It is estimated

TURNAROUND

GROUP TURNOVER (£'ooos)

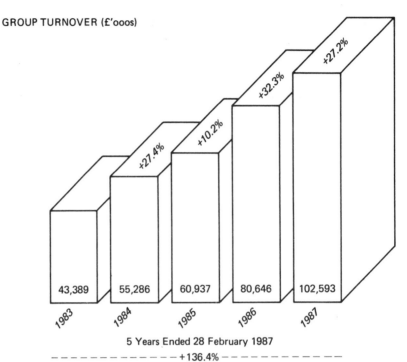

	+27.4%	+10.2%	+32.3%	+27.2%
43,389	55,286	60,937	80,646	102,593
1983	1984	1985	1986	1987

5 Years Ended 28 February 1987

— — — — — — — — — — — +136.4% — — — — — — — — — —

GROUP PROFIT BEFORE TAX (£'000s)

FIGURE 5.1 *Kwik-Fit's turnover and profits, 1983–7.*

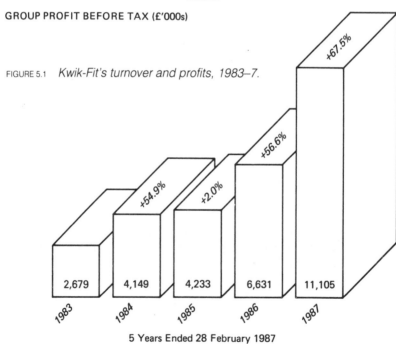

	+54.9%	+2.0%	+56.6%	+67.5%
2,679	4,149	4,233	6,631	11,105
1983	1984	1985	1986	1987

5 Years Ended 28 February 1987

— — — — — — — — — — — +314.5% — — — — — — — — — — — —

that 25 per cent of the cars now on Britain's roads are owned by companies and that 70 per cent of new cars in 1986 were registered under company names. This sector of the car aftermarket spends over £150m annually on tyres and exhausts.

As far back as 1982 Tom Farmer had signed Gelco, a company with some 20,000 cars for leasing. The computerisation of Kwik-Fit had meant that a national chain could service companies such as Gelco, and other companies with fleets, throughout the country, with just the provision of one computerised invoice from Head Office to Head Office.

In the 1987 Annual Report and Accounts Farmer was able to report that fleet customers, included, in addition to Gelco, the Ministry of Defence, Thames Water Authority, the Scottish Office, Hertz, Avis, Hotpoint, Thorn EMI, GEC, Rowntree Mackintosh, Lex and Swan National. The formation of a Kwik-Fit Fleet Division in 1987 signalled the intention to develop this business still further.

The computer-based system installed in 1982 was the third factor quoted by *The Times* in its report on the 1987 results. Farmer knew that the introduction of MAT would give him financial stock, sales and marketing data which would enable him to exert a tight control on the company. Perhaps only Tom Farmer could have anticipated how the benefits would develop over the following 5 years; and that by 1987 divisional directors and other members of senior management would have portable computers in briefcases which they could plug in from almost anywhere in the chain to the mainframes at Edinburgh and obtain all the essential information needed by top management.

The 1987 report stated, 'The Group operates the most advanced computerised data collection and analysis system, enabling every level of management to scrutinise every key indicator of the Company's retail operations on a daily basis'. But more than that, all credit-card payments to credit-card companies, including transactions on the company's own 'Autocharge Card', are processed daily. Credit accounts, invoices and statements are updated daily. The company's computers are linked with suppliers' computers and stock orders are transmitted automatically. Payroll and the transfer of money into employees' accounts and all other accounting reporting and analysis is now done by the MAT system. 'Kwik-Fit operates a fast and efficient trading environment where paperwork is kept to a minimum, allowing centre staff and management to concentrate on improving sales and profitability through attention to customers needs,' said the 1987 report.

The company's aim, as Farmer has been saying for year after year, not just in the reports but on the walls of every depot throughout the country and plastered in letters almost a foot high, is '100 per cent customer satisfaction'. In 1986 it received fewer than two complaints per 10,000 customers, confirming that the Customer Care Programme ensures that Kwik-Fit customers receive the standards of quality, reliability and service which they are entitled to expect.

In 1985 Scotland's Livingston Industrial and Commercial Association created Tom Farmer a 'Captain of Industry'. He joined an illustrious group of 'Captains', which includes Sir Monty Finniston, Sir Freddie Laker, Sir Lawrie Barratt and Sir Trevor Holdsworth.

The *Independent* of 27 March 1987, under the headline 'Courtesy pays for Kwik-Fit', wrote, 'Kwik-Fit's recipe for success – trained, courteous staff and efficient service at a reasonable price, SOMETHING MOTORISTS ARE NOT USED TO – is paying off'.

The annual conference on 31 May 1987, described by *Motor Trader* as the 'Kwik-Fit evangelical meeting', was attended by some 720 members of staff, including a massive contingent of staff from The Netherlands and Belgium, suppliers, investors, analysts, consultants, and interested parties from as far afield as the United States and Japan. Farmer there proclaimed his ambition: to make Kwik-Fit into an international group which would look after the car from the moment it was bought until the moment it was scrapped. 'I have a dream,' he said, 'of Kwik-Fit being the dominant force in the UK repair market – and in many other countries as well.' 'If Tom Farmer had been a preacher,' wrote *Motor Trader*, 'he would have had no problems converting people to his religion. As it is . . . he must have converted many to his business philosophy.'

That philosophy has been remarkably consistent from the beginning. As far back as 1972 Farmer had written, 'At Kwik-Fit, the most important person is the customer and it must be the aim of us all to give 100 per cent customer satisfaction 100 per cent of the time . . . We at Kwik-Fit recognise that our employees are our most valuable asset . . . they are the all-important contact with the customers and they are the key to the success of the Kwik-Fit Group. . .'

The loudest cheer at the conference followed Tom Farmer's reference to the breaking of the £100m turnover and £10m profit barriers and his setting of the £200m turnover target. For the half year ended 31 August 1987, the group, under its new name Kwik-Fit Holdings plc, announced a turnover rise from £51.7m to £62.9m, and a pre-tax profit of £8m. This comfortably exceeded, by more than 20 per cent, the group profit for the whole of the 1986 financial year.

As the company moved into 1988 so it continued to dominate sectoral news on all fronts.

In January, Kwik-Fit won the British Midland Diamond Award for 'Promise Fulfilment', the citation stating, 'The company's commitment to the customer is reflected in its massive success in an industry which often has a poor reputation.'

A week later, Tom Farmer announced yet another demonstration of the company's social responsibility: this time a major initiative in the interests of child safety. Selected Kwik-Fit depots offered correctly fitted child safety seats at a discounted price, to be refunded when the seat was returned once the child outgrew it. Parliamentary Under-Secretary of State for Transport, Peter Bottomley, said: 'The imaginative and generous initiative launched by Kwik-Fit will help in a most practical way to save lives and prevent injuries.'

Yes, there had been a blip in Kwik-Fit's progress in 1982. The turn-around had been accomplished. At the end of February 1988, as a new financial year began, Kwik-Fit had grown to 400 outlets, the target for 1990. The company would continue to grow provided it fulfilled its promise of 100 per cent customer satisfaction – and that meant the sort of personal dedication which Farmer could rely on from colleagues such as Greg Dolan, Tony Dolan, Tommy Hughson and Jim Robertson, who had all worked with him in the early 1970s. Who would be bold enough to predict that Tom Farmer's aim of Kwik-Fit being the 'dominant force in the UK repair and servicing market' is too ambitious to be accomplished in his lifetime?

6 The Enka Group

by Josef R. Hutter,
President, THE ENKA GROUP

The last 15 years have been a turbulent period in the history of all man-made fibre (MMF) producers. The industry moved from a situation of rapid growth and healthy profits to one of stagnation or decline and life-threatening losses. After almost 10 years of nearly constant losses, the pendulum began swinging back at the beginning of the 1980s and the cycle has turned to profitability again.

This rough scenario covers all man-made fibre producers. The Enka group, although the largest European chemical fibre manufacturer, can be seen only as an example for the entire industry. The strategy for mastering the crisis that worked for Enka must be seen only as an example for crisis management. The path Enka took worked in hindsight, but no general validity can be claimed. At the depth of the crisis, there was certainly no guarantee that it would even work for Enka.

The Enka group of companies forms a division of the Dutch chemical concern Akzo. In 1973, shortly before the crisis began, Enka was mainly engaged in the production of chemical fibres for apparel and home textiles. In fact in that year 57 per cent of sales came from those applications. A further 23 per cent came from man-made fibres for industrial applications and only 20 per cent from non-fibre products (plastics, machines and others). From these numbers one can already get a feeling of the susceptibility of the group. Standing on one leg has never been a very secure foundation.

Up until the beginning of the 1970s the demand for man-made textile fibres in Europe grew rapidly. This was due to the high growth in consumption of clothing and home textiles on the one hand and to substitution of natural fibres on the other. Optimistic prognoses of future growth led to capacity expansions that were facilitated by productivity increases, technological advances and, in some instances, subsidies. In the years that followed, the growth rate of the world economy slowed considerably, with the result that the consumption of textiles also slowed. In addition to that, imports of textiles to Western Europe increased considerably and turned a balanced import/export situation in 1970 into an import surplus of 600,000 tonnes by 1976, in spite of the much-touted multi-fibre agreements.

The discrepancy between production capacities and consumption became evident after a raw material shortage (oil) led to excessive market demand at the beginning of 1974. In the summer of 1974 the market collapsed.

The results of this development were catastrophic:

- At a time in which a seasonal upswing normally occurs, shipments of man-made fibres actually dropped by 30–40 per cent.

- The effect of this decline was that the industry entered the most serious crisis in its history with extremely high inventories.

- Sales prices fell markedly. The price index for synthetic fibres (1970 = 100), which stood at 94 in the summer of 1974, fell to 77 within a very short period.

- The costs of production (especially energy, raw materials and wages) remained at a high level or continued rising.

- The financial condition of the industry turned from 'highly profitable' to 'highly loss-making' almost overnight. Losses incurred by the industry in Europe amounted to around 20 per cent of sales in 1975.

Table 6.1 gives an impression of the seriousness of the situation.

In the 8 years from 1975 to 1982 only 1979 showed a marginally positive result. That year was followed by the second oil price shock, which sent energy and raw material prices skyrocketing and the world economy into depression. Altogether in this period the European man-made fibre producers lost the phenomenal sum of 14 billion DM, of which Enka's share was about 10 per cent.

The steps taken by Enka to overcome this crisis began in 1974. They can be divided into three categories according to their priority: the short-term safeguarding of liquidity; secondly, the medium-term exit from products whose losses were of a structural nature, and measures to

TABLE 6.1   *Enka Group (consolidated figures in millions of DM)*

	1973	1975	1979	1980	1985	1986
MMF production (000 tonnes)	480	318	436	410	409	381
Sales	3,250	2,710	3,625	3,500	4,940	4,770
Income (loss)	76	(490)	33	(315)	227	229
Investment exp.	165	180	150	222	294	387
Employees (000)	43.7	40.3	36.0	35.3	28.8	30.0

cut costs in the other areas; and, thirdly, the long-term restructuring of the company and diversification into new areas.

Measures taken to safeguard the company's liquidity of course had top priority. These included:

1 *Reducing working capital.* The sudden decrease in shipments out resulted in the accumulation of stocks of raw materials and fall-off in work in progress and inventories quickly got out of proportion. If stocks were to be reduced, several million DM could be freed for other purposes. One way in which this could be effected would be by dealing more promptly with outstanding claims. This had posed a problem during the boom period. Once a speedy despatch of orders had been established, the criterion 'Sales Outstanding' was lowered considerably.

2 *Measures in personnel.* Since shipments of man-made fibres remained on a low level for quite some time, production had to be reduced even further. In some instances this led to rates of capacity utilisation of less than 50 per cent. At times every third employee in the MMF industry was on short time. The variable wage costs were reduced accordingly, but, due to other, rising variable costs (raw materials and energy), falling gross margins had to be accepted. In addition, the fixed wage costs (collective bargaining contracts) continued rising. A further step in this period was to stop hiring. Through normal fluctuation this led to a reduction in the number of employees.

3 *Spreading of investments.* One of the most difficult steps taken was

the decision to reduce investment. Not only were no new investments approved, but also orders for previously approved investments were not fulfilled. In 1976 investment expenditures reached an all-time low of 75 million DM (less than 2.5 per cent of sales!) and were for a number of years less than depreciation. This was a difficult but effective way of safeguarding liquidity, although obviously only on a short-term basis. The first criterion for approving investments in that period was the expected near-term negative effects of putting them off and only in the second place the importance of the investment for strategic purposes.

4 *Other steps*. Efforts to find some relief in raw-material costs were most difficult, mainly because synthetic fibre raw materials only make up a small percentage of the petrochemical product mix and the demand for other petrochemical raw materials remained at a high level. Around 1977 raw-material costs did begin to decline, but the decline was coupled with a renewed decrease in sales prices. The short-term effects of other steps (for example, cuts in travel and telephone costs or other expenses) should not be underestimated here, but their impact was mainly on the psychological atmosphere in the company.

Medium-term steps taken were geared towards returning the Enka Group to profitability. An important instrument in this respect was strategic planning. For years before the crisis the strategic planning department at Enka was engaged in determining which products in which quantities and in which geographical areas should form part of the company's product mix. A handy tool for this endeavour was found in the portfolio technique. This well-known methodology analyses a product according to the combination of its (external) industry attractiveness and its (internal) business strength. After positioning all the strategic business units according to these two criteria in a matrix, it analyses the portfolio in view of the balance between growth products, cash generators, products with innovative potential and products that are structurally unprofitable. The medium-term goal, then, was to safeguard the cash generators through cost reduction and product improvement. But it was found necessary to abandon certain products whose losses were of a structural nature.

1 *Abandoning loss-making products*. The biggest structural problem

in Europe at that time was one of over-capacity. This problem ensued partly from the growth philosophy of the 1960s and partly from the rapid technological progress that made capacity expansions so inexpensive. In addition, employment considerations (in a capital intensive industry!) led to government subsidies in some countries. Needless to say the growth prognoses did not fulfil themselves and Europe experienced stagnation in textiles coupled with increasing imports. Movements in foreign exchange rates, especially the US dollar, were also not helpful.

The same problem viewed from a different angle was the so-called 'palette theory', held by fibre producers. According to this theory, a supplier of fibres had to offer all man-made fibres in his product mix if he was to be taken seriously by the customers. It goes without saying that it was impossible, especially in a situation of excess capacities, to build up a sufficiently strong, and profitable, position in all fibres to stick to this theory for very long.

Enka was one of the first companies to recognise the dark clouds on the horizon and already in 1972 started an attempt at structural change. Socio-political factors, however, prevented any sweeping changes: the actual crisis had not yet begun! By 1975 the situation had changed dramatically.

The first step toward medium-term structural improvements began with teams of qualified employees analysing market expectations and competitiveness, as well as the strategic importance of the various products according to uniform standards. The priority list drawn up by this procedure was basically the same as that found in the strategic planning. The list also made clear where capacity adaptations were necessary and where profitability could be substantially improved by cost reduction or specialisation.

After these aspects were clarified, discussions with employee representatives began. The scepticism about the necessity and correctness of these measures that came up again and again in these discussions was at least moderated by the continuing calamity in the textile fibres market and by analyses by external sources. (External sources are suited for checking the correctness of decisions 'one more time', and are also one adequate means of defending decisions in public. The actual decisions to be made and steps to be taken are, however, those of the management and it is important that this be unambiguously known, both inside and outside the firm.)

In the latter half of the 1970s Enka set about tackling both aspects of the over-capacities problem. Of the original twenty-nine European plants for textile and carpet fibres (outside Spain), eighteen were closed or transferred. Capacities were reduced by about 50 per cent, and the number of employees was reduced accordingly. The other aspect of the over-capacities problem – the 'palette theory' – was solved by Enka giving up products where it either had a small position or, owing to the cost structure, the product was unprofitable and likely to remain so. These products included rayon, acrylic and nylon staple fibres and, more recently, nylon textile filament yarns. Currently Enka's traditional fibres are limited to all types of polyester, nylon and rayon filament yarns for textile and industrial applications, and nylon carpet yarns.

With the help of transfers within the company and early retirement, but also with dismissals in conjunction with social plans, the consequences of personnel reductions could be moderated. The costs of these social plans and the special allowances for plant closures, however, led to even higher losses in an already dismal period (1975 and 1980, the two worst years, with losses of 490m and 315m DM, contained special provisions of 240m DM and 246m DM, respectively).

One important aspect with respect to plant closures and abandoning products was the timing. On the one hand fixed-cost reductions had to take place before the margins supplied by those products stopped flowing. This was at least partially achieved by beginning as early as possible to reduce fixed costs while maintaining production of the product to be abandoned for as long as possible. On the other hand, timing was important for reducing the social costs and lay-off problems involved with plant closures. By gradually effecting the necessary changes and extending them over a period of time, Enka kept these as low as possible.

2 *Additional measures to reduce fixed costs.* Parallel to abandoning structurally loss-making products a programme to reduce fixed costs throughout the entire company, including research and development, was implemented. Since personnel costs represent the lion's share of fixed costs, action taken in this area was mostly concentrated on personnel, and therefore it was necessary to reduce fixed costs in this area by a larger amount than that brought about by reductions in production.

The first step in this area was an across-the-board percentage reduction in all non-production areas. Since the crisis continued longer than expected, it then became necessary to analyse each department in the search for ways to cut costs further. The main criterion here was the strategic importance of each area to the survival of the company. As with reductions in personnel in association with plant closures, the reductions made here were carried out with the help of transfers and early retirement as much as possible in order to keep the social consequences to a minimum.

These steps were all the more difficult as it became necessary, in spite of a general hiring stoppage, to begin bringing younger people into the organisation. The first years of the hiring stoppage had led to a shift in the age structure of the company's employees. In order to secure the future management of the group and to prevent a potentially dangerous 'greying' of the management, younger persons had to be hired at the same time as reductions were still taking place elsewhere.

3 *Industry-wide measures.* Enka of course was not alone in all of this. The problem was a European one and all European man-made fibre producers were affected. To be included in these medium-term steps are the two so-called Brussels agreements whereby the major producers in Europe got together and worked out capacity reductions. Within the framework of these agreements European man-made fibre capacities were reduced by almost 1 million tonnes, or 20 per cent. The agreements are without parallel in other industries.

4 *Other measures.* In continuation of the short-term steps, working capital had to be kept under careful control and even further reduced. In addition, Enka began negotiating raw-material contracts in order to attain the best possible terms for purchases as well as to achieve a certain amount of stability in prices. In today's competitive marketplace these steps for surviving a crisis have of course become part of a regular programme for securing and improving profitability.

Carrying out these medium-term plans was, as can be imagined, an extremely difficult task. It was during this period that Enka's image in the press and in the public suffered most. Headlines concerning Enka carried little more than continued losses and plant closures. In the meantime, and in anticipation of the conclusion, it can be said that with the return of profitability came a return of a better image. Fortunately time does heal all wounds.

As soon as the short- and medium-term plans had entered the implementation phase, the company's management could turn again to the fundamental considerations of the long-term strategy. In this area the company's dependence on the problem-ridden textile and carpet fibres was of importance. Diversification became the name of the game, and it became important to choose areas related to either Enka's product or market knowledge, or preferably both.

In order to facilitate understanding of these long-term aspects we must describe the Enka group in a little more detail at this point. The basis of Enka's activities is its experience and know-how in polymer technologies. The group had its origins around the turn of the last century with the first man-made fibres made from cellulose. In the course of this century the synthetic fibres and the engineering plastics based thereon, were added to the product mix. A natural offshoot of Enka's traditional business was machines for the textile, man-made fibre and plastics industries.

As mentioned earlier, the actual product mix 15 years ago was biased towards man-made fibres and, within this group, especially towards bulk fibres for clothing and home textiles. The long-term goal then was to effect a shift in the business mix towards more sophisticated products and towards markets that required marketing expertise. The relative share of bulk textile fibres had to be reduced in favour of products with higher growth rates and higher value added, while not leaving Enka's polymer basis. Looking back with the 20/20 vision of hindsight, we can say that Enka chose a three-pronged approach towards a long-term strategy.

The first prong was to return to a profitable position in clothing and home textile fibres. How this was achieved has been the subject of much of this chapter. Capacities were shut down, and products where Enka had little experience or that were structurally unprofitable were dropped. For long-term profitability Enka concentrated on those speciality products and market niches that required the production and marketing expertise built up over the decades. These were polyester for clothing and home textiles, viscose filament for clothing, and speciality nylon bulked continuous filament (BCF) carpet yarns mainly for contract sector carpeting (schools, offices, hospitals, etc.). Although considerable sums were and are being invested in modernising these products, they form the 'cash cows' that provide the financial resources for diversification in other areas.

The second strategic group of products was man-made fibres for such industrial applications as tyre and rubber reinforcement, ropes, nets, sewing yarns, tarpaulins, and safety belts. Unlike textile fibres, these industrial fibres showed (and continue to show) satisfactory growth rates. More importantly, however, they require production and research expertise that practically exclude 'me too' manufacturers. Today Enka is one of the two largest producers of fibres for industrial applications and, with the recent introduction of the high-technology carbon and aramid fibres, has the widest product range.

The third group of products that formed the basis of a financially healthy Enka can be disrespectfully lumped together under 'others'. It consists of Enka's machine factories, previously mentioned, as well as such other polymer products as engineering plastics and compounds, non-woven materials and membranes for medical and industrial applications. This group of products provided much of the growth achieved in recent years and will continue to do so in the future. In each of them Enka already holds leading positions in their markets or market segments.

Today, although far from satisfied with the present product mix, Enka has a healthy structure, with one-third of sales coming from each of the three groups of products.

In the marketplace Enka presents itself basically as a technically competent problem-solver. It goes without saying that, against this background, application technologies and expert customer service are of immense importance.

The focal point of Enka's product differentiation is placed on specialities and market niches. This is a trend that can be widely observed. Homogeneous mass markets that were once the objective of business activities are slowly dissolving into a large number of market niches. Higher purchasing power and a stronger quality consciousness on the part of the customer form the other side of the coin. Growing leisure, tourist or telecommunication industries stimulate the emergence of entirely new markets. This trend will continue.

The internal organisational structure must also be adapted to these changes. This holds for Enka for two reasons. First, the crisis and survival attitudes have to be redirected towards a growth and differentiation scenario. Secondly, the specialisation and market-niche strategy requires a withdrawal from large and mostly functionally oriented units and a movement towards smaller groups with more broadly defined responsibilities. Organisation theories have also changed in this direction. In this way entrepreneurial self-initiative can be fostered, with the result that personnel are more motivated and can identify better with their work and with the company.

In conclusion it can be said that Enka's diversification, together with the rejuvenated traditional business areas, was the key to its success in returning to its former position as a financially healthy group. In general it can be said – at least for Enka – that these efforts were most successful where new products based on areas related to Enka's traditional technologies and markets were introduced. New products for entirely new markets often did not lead to the results hoped for. This statement of course cannot be considered an absolute truth, but, based on experience, Enka will stick to it. After all, Enka did pay a healthy price for that experience.

by Rebecca Nelson

'We are a very different company now than we were five years ago in terms of profits and profitability, and in terms of objectives and strategies. We are also more complex, more widely spread, and more decentralised.' Denys Henderson was referring to the UK-based chemical multinational ICI.

Approaching his retirement, Sir John Harvey-Jones had declared, 'There have been changes and those have gone close to my highest realistic hopes.' What remains uncertain, however, is how enduring these changes will be. That won't be known for some time yet. Nevertheless the ICI of the late 1980s is a more accessible company, more competitive, quicker and more consistent in its decision-making than ever before.

To a great extent the story of ICI is synonymous with that of the world chemical industry as a whole. For many years market growth was virtually irrepressible, and the industry was propelled by technology and capacity. The modern petrochemicals industry, with huge complexes developed in the 1960s, soon took up fibres and plastics, with similar growth patterns.

By the early 1960s ICI was a world-ranking chemicals business, and the UK economy was in a bad way. The management at ICI realised the company could no longer depend so completely upon a faltering UK economy. Despite the competition, Western Europe was the best choice for expansion. The Treaty of Rome provided the company with the leverage it needed to formulate plans for a concerted launch on the EEC. By the mid-1960s a new division, ICI Europa, had been created in Brussels, designed to share the burden of market development with the UK divisions and ease them into Europe.

ICI's expansion into the US market had been limited to a few minor acquisitions and joint ventures until 1971, when it bought Atlas, a medium-sized producer of 'effect' chemicals and pharmaceuticals. This acquisition was a fine addition to ICI's fast-growing pharmaceuticals division, and provided the company with the US expansion it had desired.

But ICI, in common with most of its competitors, was in line to become one of the casualties. It had developed into a production-oriented company – a bias rewarded in times of economic growth but severely penalised during times of recession.

Such consumer products as specialist chemicals and pharmaceuticals were obvious developments from the technology base, but sometimes such developments got out of hand. ICI moved outside its main area of expertise. Because it produced paints, decorative materials and plastics, the company branched out into the do-it-yourself retailing sector, even setting up a building development group. And money was lost.

For years, ICI had been governed by a succession of autocratic chairmen. The first, Lord McGowan, was ensconced in the chair for 24 years. Sir Paul Chambers continued the tycoon tradition from 1960 to 1968. It was he who showed contempt for ICI's culture in ways that live on in the memory of those still working there. When his attempted takeover bid for Courtaulds resulted in a bitter defeat, he introduced McKinsey & Co. to advise on a corporate reorganisation.

Sir Paul's term of office was the catalyst for change. New systems were developed in an attempt to establish a democratic way of electing the chairman but these didn't prove very effective. During the 1970s four chairmen were appointed; not only were they all approaching retirement, but they tended to be conservative choices too. Such conservatism was also apparent in the insularity of each director, convinced that what was good for his division was good for ICI. Nobody stood for the interests of the organisation as a whole.

The management style may seem dated now, but throughout this period, when there was a cautious choice of chairman, plus conservatism among the directors, profits were booming! They rose from £148m, pre-tax, in 1971 to £613m in 1979.

Naturally, this convinced ICI it was right to pursue this strategy of unbridled spending and expansion; and in keeping with its competitors, it continued unrestrainedly to build commodity chemical plants. After all, there seemed no reason to change tack.

ICI began the 1970s intent on growing considerably faster in non-commodity products – 'effect' chemicals, which are valued according to the effect they produce – than in commodity, or 'heavy', chemicals. But the need simultaneously to maintain a position in commodities meant that these operations developed a momentum of their own. During the 1970s ICI went on a capital-spending spree to the tune of approximately £4 billion. 'We knew we needed more growth in the effect end of the business,' says new chairman Denys Henderson. 'We began the decade with 70 per cent of our assets in heavy chemicals and 30 per cent in effect businesses. Then years later it was still 70:30. The strategy was there. What was not so hot was the implementation.' It was the losses on commodities from the previous decade that were largely to blame for ICI's troubles in the early 1980s.

Along came the second oil crisis in 1979 and brought this uncontrolled expansion in commodity chemicals to a sudden halt. In the autumn of 1980 ICI announced its third-quarter results early: they were dreadful. The company recorded its first ever pre-tax losses, which amounted to £16m. In a desperate attempt to conserve cash ICI cut its dividend, for the first time since the 1930s, from 23p a share to 17p. To this day some people in the City have never forgiven them for this action. But as Brian Smith, a former executive director, points out, 'Let's be quite clear, the events of 1980 and 1981 scared us to bloody death.'

Petrochemicals, plastics, fibres and colours were the sectors most severely hit. Each recorded losses for three consecutive years. Even profits from usually healthy sectors, such as agriculture, pharmaceuticals and oil, could not stem the impact of so great a loss for ICI. The whole company looked on the brink of disaster.

By now, with the benefit of hindsight, ICI may have wished it had concentrated more on 'effect' chemicals. As oil prices rose during ICI's bumper year of 1979, the company became aware of the gloomy outlook for chemicals and began to cut back on capital expenditures. Even so, investment remained at an exceptionally high level, reflecting the optimism of earlier years. While over £430m went into plant expansion in 1979 and 1980, the recession sent ICI's business plummeting. The healthy pound exacerbated the company's troubles. The UK was still the source of at least half ICI's manufacturing assets, and as a rule, the company exported about half its UK output. However, as Britain's oil production developed, the pound became one of the world's petrocurrencies. Between 1979 and its peak in 1981 it appreciated nearly 30 per cent against the deutsche mark, the home currency of ICI's major German competitors, Bayer, BASF and Hoechst, and left the company at a disadvantage.

A modest recovery occurred in 1981, but divisional losses continued for another year or so, especially in the petrochemicals and plastics sectors. Everything shipped from Britain was losing money, said former director Brian Smith. The profits slide continued relentlessly, particularly in the petrochemicals and plastics sectors, falling to a 10-year low point of £139m pre-tax in 1982, due in part to heavy redundancy costs. These problems provided a uniquely turbulent backdrop for the election of ICI's next chairman.

Mere talk of change was not enough now. A new and perhaps more assertive spirit was needed. In 1981 ICI's democratic method of selecting its leader faced its first real challenge.

The choice of Sir John Harvey-Jones, the flamboyant and independently minded deputy chairman, as leader of ICI heralded a dramatic departure from what had been the norm since 1968. John Harvey-Jones was too much the advocate of change to concur fully with the shared values of the managers, whose collective sensibility was offended by the concept of the chairman as CEO. Once appointed, the chairman previously had remained, in essence, *primus inter pares*.

However, Harvey-Jones' appointment in 1982 was proof of the ultimate discernment of the election system at ICI. It proved that, when in dire straits, the board could choose a strong leader and arm him with the time and the means to do the job. Harvey-Jones was appointed for 5 years, as opposed to the customary 3, and with the help of the retiring chairman, Sir Maurice Hodgson, who had objected to the limits of his own authority, he managed to win much greater power. Not least amongst these was the acknowledgement that the new chairman would also be 'principal executive officer'. The chairman wanted a greater role in hiring and firing members of the board, and to have a say in all their salaries.

Harvey-Jones was just the candidate to cope with a turbulent future. He was clear and outspoken, with an avant-garde taste in ties. He was an advocate of change and commitment, and an open critic of the company systems. Before, the emphasis at ICI had been on decisions, but from 1982 it was to be on action. Said one executive, 'He was seen as the man who perceived the need for change most clearly and who was most likely to carry it out.' He did indeed realise it was vital to implement changes early on if he was to transform and regenerate a corporate behemoth.

In the five years of Harvey-Jones' chairmanship ICI underwent considerable change as he implemented his turnaround strategy. These changes affected the size, organisation, product base and geographical balance of the business. But it should not be overlooked that, compared with the early 1980s, the chemical industry worldwide has been in a state of relative calm, and a healthier worldwide economy has helped make the turnaround possible.

John Harvey-Jones recalled the vast payroll of the 1960s and 1970s, which had been a yardstick by which ICI was measured unfavourably against its competition. He said, 'The volume of output had shrunk dramatically and the only way to improve productivity was to get rid of vast numbers of people.' This is exactly what he did. Between 1979 and 1984 ICI slashed its workforce. In Britain alone it was cut by a third, to 58,000. But sales per employee during this period increased from £36,221 to £85,718, and ICI's profits per employee went from £3,907 in 1979 to £8,945 in 1984.

Since 1982 ICI has deliberately moved away from petrochemicals, plastics, general chemicals and fibres and towards the profit-earners of the future: pharmaceuticals, advanced materials, electronics, medical diagnostics and crop applications from bio-science. This has had a remarkable effect on profits: the new industries had formerly contributed 56 per cent of them, but now they account for 68 per cent. The ratio of heavy chemicals to effect chemicals is now 46:54. So, by reducing overheads and shifting the emphasis away from heavy chemicals, Harvey-Jones was steering ICI along a course of increasing profitability.

Because ICI's survival depended on moving into areas of high-tech and high growth, Harvey-Jones spent over £700m in 1985–6 on acquisitions in higher-margin, higher-growth 'speciality' businesses, and he steadily boosted research spending. In pursuing this philosophy, he moved ICI away from Britain and into stronger markets abroad. But, as Harvey-Jones admitted, 'We want a company that will make lots of money when things go well, but isn't exposed to horrible losses when things go badly. We're willing to forgo the sirens of heaven to avoid the fires of hell.'

In pursuit of his pledge Harvey-Jones probably acquired more businesses for ICI in his first 9 months as chairman than the company had done in the previous 9 years. It snapped up 35 firms in 1986 alone, bringing the total to around 100 in 3 years. However, Harvey-Jones was careful to avoid buying into unrelated areas, and to this end ICI keeps an international databank on all the companies in the industry.

In October 1984 ICI set up the Acquisitions Team (or 'A-Team', as it was known), comprising four executives led by the Main Board Director at that time, Denys Henderson. Its brief was to review potential acquisitions and, when the time was right, to act fast. Its efficiency was apparent when Beatrice Foods' chemicals division became available. In the space of one day the team had moved the entire operation to New York. ICI's bid of US$750m was then accepted in December 1984, and ICI added about US$450m to its US sales for 1985.

ICI's acquisition rate totally dwarfs that of many of its rivals. Most of the company's purchases, however, are so smoothly initiated that they receive little publicity. The cost of the Garst deal, when completed in the autumn of 1984, has never been disclosed. A private US firm, Garst gave ICI the opportunity to apply its bio-science expertise in the development of new strains of seeds. Genetically engineered plants resulting from this and similar link-ups are unlikely to be on the market in significant quantities for at least 15 years. Harvey-Jones explains that he bought Garst when he did because, 'Increasingly, the effects produced by ferti-lisers will be concentrated in the production of the plant itself. If you have a plant which can fix its own nitrogen, you don't need to chuck lots of fertilisers on the ground.' Incidentally, ICI's sales of fertilisers and agri-chemicals are worth more than £1.8 billion a year, yielding profits of more than £200m annually.

This type of rationale has led the company to develop PET, the raw material used in plastic-bottle manufacturing – a logical step when one of its bulk chemical markets is soda ash for glass bottlers. 'If we don't, somebody else will,' says Harvey-Jones. It is rare for ICI to buy a company to acquire its R&D; almost always it has bought market posi-tion, so that it can apply what it already knows.

The business accomplishments of the Harvey-Jones period – retrenchment, rationalisation, growth by acquisition – are not always easy to attribute to individuals: collective decision-making is still a strong feature of ICI, particularly at the top. 'On major issues,' an executive director explains, 'if more than two people are against a proposal, the majority are unlikely to take it forward – although they might try again later.' There were occasions when Harvey-Jones over-rode the wishes of the majority, but these were few and far between.

Nevertheless Harvey-Jones' notable personal achievement was to improve the efficiency of the board. His strategy for broadening ICI's geographical spread included adding foreign, non-executive directors to the board, a move which would have been unthinkable in the 1970s, when conformity to established practice was gospel at ICI. The addition of West German insurance chief Walther Kiep is an indication of ICI's increasing commitment to the European market. Furthermore, although most of ICI's bulk raw material purchases are dollar-denominated, it is the deutsche mark which is its main currency denominator for sales.

South-east Asia and Japan are major expansion targets for all chemical companies. In an attempt to break into this difficult market ICI appointed Toshiba's Shoichi Saba (who has since resigned as Chairman of Toshiba) to the board. Obviously the advantages of such a relationship with a man who also ran a multinational with £10 billion annual sales were manifold.

Harvey-Jones' sweeping alterations to the board entailed more than simply the appointment of non-executive directors from overseas companies. He shook ICI to its roots by decentralising the company, cutting out an entire level of senior executives. Having once described ICI's sprawling empire as having 'divisions like dogs have fleas', he set about reducing the numbers of the executive team from the earlier dozen or more to seven – simply by not replacing retiring members. This created a closer-working team, which in turn was quicker and more efficient.

Before the Harvey-Jones era each director at ICI had two or three different roles; these might have included duties of a personnel nature, duties in a particular geographic area and duties in a business sector. In this last capacity, although the director oversaw his sector and acted as adviser to the UK divisional chairman, he did not take responsibility for the performance of the division.

Obviously a decision on, for example, an investment requiring technology transfer from the UK to an overseas plant would need the attention of several directors. In the 1970s the directors for such related businesses as plastics and fibres gathered in 'policy groups under a deputy chairman. This led to very powerful factions developing inside the boardroom, as every director was an advocate for his own division of business.

The function of Harvey-Jones' more compact board is, he says, 'to work on the future of the corporation as a whole rather than the individual bits . . . The responsibility is to manage the board.'

In February 1985 ICI was the first British industrial company to announce pre-tax profits of over £1 billion for the previous year. That was followed by an 8 per cent fall-off, although sales did pass the £10 billion mark. Then in February 1987 ICI regained its premier position when it announced its pre-tax profits of £1.016 billion for the previous year, with a share price at just under £14, its highest ever level. This served as a perfect swansong for Sir John Harvey-Jones, as he prepared to step down after saving ICI from collapse.

The company he left behind in April 1987 was radically different from the one he inherited in April 1982. When he took over the helm, ICI, 'the supertanker', was heading for the rocks. Severely damaged by the recession and the second oil crisis, it looked like becoming Britain's biggest industrial casualty instead of her biggest manufacturing company. Since then ICI has sailed well on course, becoming one of the world's most profitable chemicals companies. Yet to the dismay of all who have worked for this stupendous turnaround, the company is still rated at a significant discount to the average of the FT index. The reasons for this, Harvey-Jones thinks, is that 'People still don't see ICI as an exciting company. We're seen as rather dull, part of the establishment. But we are an exciting company – very exciting.'

The fruits of Harvey-Jones' turnaround at ICI show clearly how much a company is governed by the dictates of the economy. It was heavy chemicals that were most exposed to external factors, such as oil price rises and currency fluctuations, and which dragged the company down so severely in 1979–80. Ironically, it was the plastics and petrochemicals business, which had clocked up a cool £96m profit in 1985, that showed a dramatic improvement to around £200m in February 1987, largely because oil was cheaper by then and currencies had been moving in the right direction.

In the calamitous year 1980 bulk products accounted for 52 per cent of sales; now they account for more like 40 per cent. Effect chemicals have boosted their share of the sales from 38 per cent to 48 per cent in the same period.

Despite the tremendous corporate recovery, ICI is taking no chances. In 1986, in an effort to create further economies by sharing overheads, it merged its heavy chemicals businesses into the ICI Chemicals and Polymers Group, based at Runcorn. The Group includes petro-chemicals, plastics, general chemicals, fibres and fertilisers. As Harvey-Jones himself pointed out, 'In commodity chemicals we can't do anything clever. If you make soda ash, you make soda ash; it's very difficult to differentiate. So it's a cost game rather than a cleverness game.'

ICI has now become less dependent on the UK, realising finally that profits could be increased by overseas expansion. In 1987 ICI was manufacturing in forty countries. US sales were up from 15 per cent to 22 per cent and are still growing. In 1985 ICI acquired Beatrice Chemicals for US$750m, and in 1986 Glidden's North American paint operations for US$580m. ICI is now the world's largest paint producer, and the Dulux brand name is a familiar sight throughout Britain.

Additionally, ICI acquired the Stauffer Chemical Company in 1987 for US$1.69 billion, and sold the speciality chemicals business of Stauffer for US$625m to Akzo. Fitting admiration comes from Joseph Salvani, a chemical analyst at Goldman, Sachs & Co. 'ICI's US business is what almost every US chemical company would like its whole business to look like.' Denys Henderson's verdict: 'I'd still like more.'

By Spring 1987 Harvey-Jones was convinced that he had turned ICI into a company as competitive as any other chemicals firm in the world. 'There are a whole number of ways of measuring competitiveness. But in terms of the things we control – manning, overheads, technical efficiency – we are among the best.'

There is no doubt that when Sir John Harvey-Jones headed for retirement in March 1987, he left on a high note. 'We've got our pride back at ICI,' he said. 'We're now knocking spots off the international competition. And you try and list the number of other British companies who are actually feared by the competition.' However, no matter how successful a company has become, it can always fall prey to outside pressure. The real measure of the turnaround at ICI – of the direction, adequacy and durability of the changes – will appear if and when another fierce storm hits the industry.

8 Istituto per la Ricostruzione Industriale (IRI)

by Professor Romano Prodi, President, IRI

At one time or another Italy's government-owned Istituto per la Ricostruzione Industriale (IRI) has made just about everything – cars and ketchup, toll roads and television shows, ships and steel, burglar alarms and air-to-air missiles. What IRI has not made much of is money. Led by Romano Prodi, a professor of industrial organisation, Italy's biggest company is lurching back towards profitability. After losing more than 7,000 billion lire between 1982 and 1985, IRI earned more than 300 billion lire in 1986. This was its first profit since 1973. This chapter traces the facts and events contributing to the demise of IRI and examines the strategy that Prodi adopted in the late 1980s to propel IRI into the black.

The economic crisis of 1929 had serious consequences for the Italian banking system, which controlled a large part of Italian industry. After 4 years of state subsidies to the system, IRI was created in 1933, by Benito Mussolini, to take charge of all the liabilities of the banks. It thus became a state-owned holding company, controlling banks, industries and services, and wielding an exceptional amount of power and influence.

Alberto Beneduce, the first IRI president, apparently knew what was needed: not a nationalised group but a tool for flexible intervention on the part of the state. This is the peculiarity of the IRI formula. The Institute, or, more precisely, the holding company, is state-owned, but its companies are in effect 'joint stock companies', managed and controlled within the framework of private law.

This mixed state–private ownership assures the managers full operational freedom in principle. When they operate in competitive markets they are free to compete; when they are in a situation of natural monopoly, they are bound to efficiency and profitability by the presence of private investors among their shareholders, who have all the rights to fair dividends.

[93]

Between 1933 and 1936, IRI undertook a rationalisation of all the activities it controlled. In 1936 the new 'Legge Bancaria' (Banking Law) completed the process by limiting the activities of the banks to ordinary credit.

After 1945 IRI played a major role in the post-war industrial restructuring. It set up the national telephone system, launched state television and the national airline (1957) and controlled the construction of the toll-highway network (1961), as well as developing Italy's shipbuilding and steel industries.

In 1974 the economic crisis affecting the whole of Italy meant IRI was called in by successive governments as a rescue institute for many ailing companies. This led to the burdensome acquisition of huge losses, as IRI took several unprofitable companies under its wing in an effort to preserve jobs.

By the early 1980s IRI had become Italy's largest industrial group, consisting of 1,000 companies. By this time it controlled Europe's largest steel company, one-fifth of Italy's banking sector, the state TV network, car manufacturer Alfa Romeo, the national airline Alitalia, and 20 per cent of the nation's food-processing capacity. With 535,000 employees, it accounted for more than 3 per cent of Italy's total employment. Yet despite all these apparent assets, IRI's net losses were then as high as 8 per cent of turnover. Its debt, at 27,000 billion lire, exceeded its yearly sales. In fact IRI's net borrowing requirements were equivalent to 12 per cent of the total credit extended to Italian households and companies. If IRI collapsed, what would happen to the national economy?

In 1981, I accepted the daunting task of trying to pull IRI back from the brink. A process of economic and financial recovery soon began. In 1983, armed with the dictum 'companies must be competitive', I set up a 5-year 'recovery schedule'. I began by replacing political appointees with managers from private enterprise, and laying off surplus members of the workforce, with the result that IRI today has 60,000 fewer staff, although it still ranks second in the world, after GM, in terms of number of employees. Executives who met neither my philosophy nor the new standards were replaced – about 70 per cent of them – with tough managers who would implement my policies. Then I went on to rally Italian politicians to the cause when I began to sell off IRI assets, following the European trend towards privatisation.

The policy for recovery appears to be working. Now IRI is breaking even, just as the 'recovery schedule' runs out. The IRI Group turnover

(32.9 thousand billion lire in 1982) grew to an estimated 47.6 thousand billion lire in 1986. In this respect IRI ranks fourteenth in the world and third outside the USA. The incidence of net financial charges, which was as high as 16 per cent of turnover in 1982, has now been halved.

The situation is still improving. Today IRI has a somewhat complex organisation. As a central holding company it controls such banks as Banca Commerciale Italiana, Credito Italiano, Banco di Roma, Banco de Santo Spirito, Mediobanca and sectoral holdings. The main subholdings are Finmeccanica, Stet, Finsider, Italstat, Fincantieri, Finmare, Finsiel, and Alitalia, which in broad terms cover three operational spheres: services, manufacturing and engineering.

To give a broad idea of IRI's range in terms of services SIP covers 82 per cent of Italian telecommunications traffic, Alitalia 91 per cent of air transportation, Finmare 21 per cent of maritime transportation, and Autostrade 45 per cent of the highways. In manufacturing Finsider has 55 per cent of the total national production of steel, Fincantieri 70 per cent of shipbuilding, Ansaldo 60 per cent of power supply components, Selenia and Aeritalia 55 per cent of aerospace, Italtel 50 per cent of TLC switching, and SGS 98 per cent of microelectronics. In engineering Ansaldo covers 65 per cent of the energy sector, Italimpianti 25 per cent of the industrial sector, and the Italstat companies 17 per cent of the infrastructure and environmental protection sector.

The strategy for the recovery of such a diversified group has followed five main delineations:

1 Industrial restructuring
2 Financial restructuring
3 Privatisation
4 Partnerships
5 Internationalisation

1 *Industrial restructuring.* Important sectors such as aerospace and TLC engineering, which were losers in 1982 (Ansaldo, Aeritalia,Selenia, Italtel), are now profit-makers. Loss-making companies still exist, but they are now mainly confined to sectors in crisis all over Europe (steel, shipbuilding).

There have been changes in management and very heavy and painful cuts in employment. Senior managers who failed to meet the profit test were replaced – about 70 per cent of them. Such cuts, however, have been implemented without major litigation, due in part to skilful negotiating and a specific code of behaviour (Protocollo IRI), signed with the unions. This has made for better labour relations at IRI than at other companies. When disputes arise, for example, the workforce and management must meet several times before unions can call a strike. The result: fewer hours lost through strike action.

2 *Financial restructuring.* By 1980 the financial situation at IRI had become very critical. Cash flows, barely positive in the mid-1970s, turned almost negative during the period from 1978 to 1981. Since there was no internal generation of funds in the group, and the provision of public funds was insufficient, IRI enterprises were forced to seek external financing, mostly in dollars, in huge volume. Drastic action could not be postponed. So three basic remedies were adopted to improve IRI's financial situation.

(i) Large capital contributions were requested of the government and obtained on the basis of precise plans of recovery, allowing the start of the recapitalisation process. Today the provision of state funds has drastically decreased.

(ii) IRI slashed its debt as a percentage of sales, and relied more on domestic rather than foreign financial sources.

(iii) Funds were raised by the divestment of enterprises not considered of strategic use to IRI's activity, and by placing on the stock market shares of companies which might interest private investors.

3 *Privatisation.* The divestment of enterprises was synonymous with privatisation. Three kinds of enterprise were considered for sale. First came marginal enterprises, those not integrated with other IRI companies and therefore having no 'mission' to accomplish within the IRI group; second were companies which were loss-makers but which could be directed elsewhere; and finally we considered enterprises or even subholdings of IRI which were or could be profitable but which did not appear to be consistent with the basic long-term objectives of IRI.

My goal was to prove that if IRI was to be efficient, it should be run like a private company. Between 1983 and today, twenty-three enterprises of differing sizes, from the large Alfa Romeo to the small Ducati, from banks to glasses and washing machine producers, have been disposed of. The process of divestment slowed down somewhat in the latter part of 1985 but regained momentum in July 1986, when a wide political consensus backed the sale of Alfa Romeo. The sports-car maker had suffered from over-capacity and low productivity for some time, failing to make a profit for 10 years or more. IRI finally sold Alfa to Fiat on 1 January 1987 for an estimated 1,600 billion lire. Currently the funds raised since 1983 by divesting companies amount to approximately 1,000 billion lire (this figure excludes the sale of Alfa Romeo).

The group has sold large parts of eighteen of its companies to the public – Alitalia and the state telephone company (SIP) among them – through the Milan Stock Exchange. This stock now accounts for 22 per cent of the market's total capitalisation, with the number of companies standing at 11 per cent of the total number listed. However, the dividends the IRI companies have distributed account for 35 per cent of total dividends. Market sales have generally been used for shares held in excess of majority control, with the aim of spreading the ownership of the companies.

Three main methods were used for the placement of shares on the stock market:

(i) Listing of new companies
(ii) Placement of shares of IRI companies previously in IRI's, or its subsidiaries', portfolios
(ii) Issuing convertible bonds and warrants.

(i) The listing of new IRI companies on the stock exchange began in 1985. For some time IRI management had felt that there were a number of companies in IRI's portfolio which were ready for listing. However, the relatively depressed conditions of the domestic market had delayed the initiative. By 1985 the improvement in market conditions made the time ripe for introducing some IRI companies to the stock market. Five have been listed since July 1985: one telecommunications (Sirti), one aerospace (Aeritalia), one mortgage institution (Credito Foniario), one highway company (Autostrade), and a mechanical engineering company (Ansaldo Trasporti).

(ii) The placement of shares of companies already listed on the market amounted to over 2,100 billion lire in 1985, and to more than 800 billion in 1986. Most of the sales were made on the Italian stock market. However, major placements – 230 billion lire by Banca Commerciale Italiana, and 180 billion lire by STET – were made in 1985 on the international market. These operations have brought about a substantial shift in IRI's and its subsidiaries' share of control in these companies' capital. IRI's ownership has decreased sometimes, as in the cases of SIP, Italcable or Cementir, to a level just sufficient to retain an absolute majority.

(iii) The issuing of convertible bonds and bonds with warrants has been an indirect way of placing shares with the public for an amount (for IRI) of 600 billion lire.

These simple data are a clear description of the nature of IRI stock. It is not 'glamour' stock because of course it will never be subject to the rapid growth of a takeover, but it has been successful because it offers the long-term benefits of good dividends. Altogether the sales have raised more than 4,400 billion lire, and in each case IRI has retained management control.

4 *Partnerships*. I am very concerned about excessive global competition, particularly in high-tech businesses, and I have devoted part of the recovery programme specifically to counteracting such threats. I sought and established partnerships and joint ventures in those areas where sharing experience is crucial to entering, or maintaining a presence in the market. An interesting case in this respect has been Seiaf, a joint IBM–EL–SAG company dedicated to factory automation and to computer-integrated manufacturing.

The issue of partnership brings up the strategic issues of licensing, joint venture programmes and subcontracting. Already Aeritalia is working with the McDonnell Douglas Corporation and Boeing, while a unit of STET, IRI's telecommunications holding company, has set up a factory-automation joint venture with the International Business Machines Corporation. In December 1986 IRI's semiconductor makers, SGS, and France's Thomson agreed to form a 500 billion lire venture to develop a super memory chip. Currently under review is the merger of Italtel, the largest Italian producer of telephone and telecommunications equipment, and Fiat's Telettra, a large private company operating in a related field. The result of the merger would be Telit, which would then become one of the largest European producers of telecommunications equipment.

5 *Internationalisation.* Internationalisation is yet another line of action in the IRI strategy of recovery. In 1985 exports rose to 26 per cent of total sales, but what is more remarkable is how their distribution has changed by geographical area. While in 1981 50 per cent of IRI's exports were sent to developing countries and 42 per cent to developed ones, by 1985 the developed countries accounted for 54 per cent of the total and the developing ones had decreased to 35 per cent. Eastern Europe and China together grew from 8 per cent to 11 per cent.

The present level of internationalisation at IRI can be summarised as follows:

(i) The foreign revenues of the group are about 40 per cent of total turnover, if only the 'exportable activities' (excluding, therefore, the national telephone network and highways) are considered.

(ii) These revenues have come from 120 companies with headquarters in Italy exporting about 10,000 billion lire, and from 90 companies located abroad with sales to the tune of 2,000 billion lire.

(iii) The IRI group has minority stakes in thirty companies with headquarters abroad.

Within this framework international co-operation is vital for IRI, and we are working hard to increase it. We realise that the very nature of our manufacturing is such that IRI companies cannot survive and develop unless they reach the size and sophistication of their competitors, and generate a comparable share of the market. So we still have a difficult task to undertake. For instance, even if the proposed Fiat–Italtel deal comes to fruition, IRI will remain a small player in the game of international telecommunications, as will SGS in comparison with its American, European and Japanese semiconductor rivals.

The part state-owned leviathan is still vulnerable to political attack despite its obvious increase in strength and independence. There are Italian politicians who are still of the opinion that IRI should remain entirely in state control. Politics have affected the sale of some of IRI's companies. For example, the government blocked the planned deal to sell off SME to Olivetti's De Benedetti because Prime Minister Craxi wanted it sold to someone more supportive of his Socialist Party.

Although obstacles hinder and complicate our efforts to run IRI like a private company, there is no denying that there has been a tremendous improvement in the group's performance, and we will go on to achieve still more. Even the World Bank is participating in the turnaround: it is using IRI to counsel developing nations trying to salvage money-losing state industries.

This leads us on to consider the future of IRI, the seeds of which are already present in the trend of the last 3 years. Now IRI is even more in control of its future, which follows three directions of development: in large networks, engineering and high-tech manufacturing. To give an idea of the commitment of IRI in each one of these directions, consider that in the next 4 years Ansaldo expects a growth of 13 per cent a year, in high-tech the aerospace companies Aeritalia and Selenia should grow 20 per cent a year, and SGS in microelectronics, and Italtel in switching, 14 per cent. Back in 1981 only 28 per cent of group activities lay in the high-tech field, but by 1985 this had grown to 52 per cent. Today IRI is even considering entering the new advanced materials sector.

In 1986 the IRI companies spent over 1,400 billion lire in R&D (20 per cent more than in 1985). Although about 12,500 people are employed in this activity, this is still too few in the face of the strong competition.

These data lead back to the topic of privatisation, but with a new scope: that of significant international cooperation. IRI intends to move on, it expects from its companies great achievements in terms of growth over the next few years, but the overriding feeling is that the group cannot make it if it becomes too insular and closes up on itself.

Three black clouds still lie on the horizon. The first is unemployment. Whilst it is not much higher as an average than other European countries, it is heavily unbalanced toward the South, especially among young people.

Second is the problem of the Southern region as a whole. The Italian government is taking a new set of actions to generate economic growth in this area, and new forms of incentives should foster industrialisation, entrepreneurship, tourism and education. Many IRI companies will surely fit in this scheme of things, which is challenging and may give opportunities of renumeration too.

The third black spot is the still very high government deficit, although measures to cut back public spending are under way. On top of the deficit is a high rate of private savings in Italy (20 per cent of GNP).

Nevertheless we are confident that further developments can and will occur, because of the innate strength within the group and because of the economic climate of Italy, where the general situation is improving.

Here are five points which make me feel particularly optimistic about the future of IRI:

1 Italy has the serious threat of terrorism under control.

2 Italian inflation has decreased to manageable levels.

3 Labour problems are also under control. The hours spent striking by the average Italian worker have dropped to a quarter of the figure of 1982.

4 Exchange rates between the Italian lira and other European currencies have been fairly stable.

5 The extraordinary growth of Italy's national financial markets since 1985.

In broad terms then I am optimistic about the future of IRI and of Italy, and I see expansion and development for the companies through establishing more international links. Historically Italy has always been of interest to foreign investors. At the end of 1985 there were over 1,200 Italian companies with foreign capital, 500,000 people employed and a turnover in the region of 72,000 billion lire. This accounts for almost 7 per cent of the national total.

The 'Italian miracle' or 'new Renaissance' has been recently brought to the world's attention by the international press: privatisation, as we have seen, has been only a tool, never an end *per se*. IRI's story is proof that the irrepressible Italian spirit is strong enough to revitalise a once clumsy and ailing leviathan.

Acorn Computer Group Plc

by Alexander Reid, Chairman, OCTAGON
INVESTMENT MANAGEMENT LIMITED

Hermann Hauser and Christopher Curry, the joint founders of Acorn Computer Group plc, invited me to join the board of their company as a non-executive director at the beginning of 1984. I had just left British Telecom, after 11 years, to set up my own venture capital business (Octagon Investment Management Ltd). I knew of Acorn because I lived in Cambridge, and in early 1984 Acorn was a famous success story. Founded only 4 years earlier, it had grown from scratch in those 4 years to a turnover of more than £90m and a profit of more than £10m. It was a young company, staffed by young and very bright people. It was a privilege to be asked to join it.

For someone who had spent his previous career in British Telecom, still run very much in the manner of a large Civil Service department, Acorn presented a striking contrast. Although it had floated on the Unlisted Securities Market (USM) in the autumn of 1983, some 80 per cent of the shares were still in the hands of the two founders, who decisively controlled the company. They were both in their early thirties, full of confidence, imagination, and drive. They had gathered around them a dedicated and creative team of people, who ran the business in an informal and risk-taking style. This was producing remarkable results in terms of growth and profit.

THE BBC MICRO

The main product of Acorn was the BBC micro-computer, an immensely successful school and hobby computer, which had been developed and marketed in conjunction with the BBC, to whom a royalty was paid. At the time it was launched it was very powerful for its price, and unlike some other micro-computers it was reliable and rugged. Through the connection with the BBC, and the widespread use of the machine in schools (aided by a Government subsidy scheme), a large range of software existed for the machine.

Like Clive Sinclair (with whom Christopher Curry had worked for some years), Acorn followed a policy of subcontracting the manufacture of the machine to third parties. Initially Acorn supplied all the parts to the subcontractor, but by 1984 the subcontractors had agreed to take on the procurement of the parts, the only item coming from Acorn being the custom-built silicon chip at the heart of the machine. The distribution of this chip was closely controlled by Acorn, because it was a proprietary device, without which the machine could not be copied. By contrast, Apple (whose early computers were built entirely from standard chips) suffered serious problems with fake machines built in the Far East ('rotten apples').

This policy of contracting out manufacture had several great advantages. It avoided the managerial problems of recruiting hundreds of assembly-line workers and investing in plant and buildings. It enabled rates of production to be built up rapidly (as became necessary when the BBC micro turned out to be such a success in the market). It reduced Acorn's working capital requirements, because the subcontractors bore the cash burden of buying in the parts.

A key feature of Acorn at this time was the very strong research and development department, of more than 100 people. This had been built up by Hermann Hauser, an Austrian who had come to Cambridge University to take his PhD in the computer science department. Several of the key people in Acorn's research and development department had come from Cambridge University, with which close links were maintained.

DANGER SIGNALS

During 1984 Acorn was the darling of the industry and the City. It epitomised the new high technology industry which the UK needed for the future. It was an admirable example of university–industry co-operation, and the fact that the founders were so young added glamour.

The City analysts talked the stock up, and by the autumn of 1984 the company was capitalised on the Unlisted Securities Market at about £200m. But danger signs were beginning to be apparent to the company's management.

The danger signs were of three kinds. Firstly, the attempts to penetrate the US and German markets were not going well. In the US Acorn had sensibly decided to concentrate on the educational computer market, rather than compete head-on with Apple and IBM in the business personal computer market. However, even the educational market (in which Acorn had established such a dominant position in the UK) was very difficult to crack in the US. This was partly because of the cost and delay of adapting the machine to US technical requirements. More importantly, the decision-makers for purchasing educational computers in the US were public bodies of various kinds (at federal, state, or city level). These people, who were spending public money, naturally had an aversion to importing foreign equipment if that could be avoided. The US being the world leader in the computer industry, it must have seemed particularly odd to them to be asked to import school computers from the UK.

The second danger signal was a general softening of demand for the BBC micro and the numerous peripherals which had been designed for it. Whereas in 1982 and 1983 demand had outrun supply, and dealers were pleading for machines, the Acorn sales force had to work hard in 1984 to sell the machines – often by means of discounts and special offers of various kinds.

The third danger signal was in relation to the Electron. This had been designed as the 'young brother' of the BBC micro. At about half the price (£199 instead of £399), it was compatible in software terms with the BBC micro, and was intended as the computer the parent would buy at home for the child who used a BBC micro at school. It had been hoped to launch the Electron in time for large sales in Christmas 1983, but development delays had postponed volume production until 1984. By the time volume production was under way, it became apparent that Sinclair, with machines at less than £100, was scooping the home market, and there were signs that the Electron would be uncomfortably stranded between the cheap Sinclair machines and the expensive (but more powerful and flexible) BBC micro.

DREAM INTO NIGHTMARE

Christmas 1984 was an exciting time for Acorn. As with any home computer manufacturer, the months of November and December were critically important for sales. Because Acorn sold to dealers and high-street retailers (rather than direct to end customers), it would take a few weeks for firm sales figures to filter back to Acorn.

By mid-January 1985 the Acorn dream had turned into a nightmare. The Christmas sales had fallen some 30 per cent below expectations, and some £30m of stock had piled up in the Acorn warehouse. Worse still, Acorn had irrevocable orders in place with subcontractors to supply at least another £30m worth of computers during 1985. Acorn's cash resources, built up from historic profits and the 1984 USM flotation, had been depleted by losses in the US and Germany.

The company suddenly found itself in a desperate situation. The subcontractors were pressing for payment for the goods already delivered to Acorn's warehouse; the dealers and high-street retailers were not ordering, as they were still overstocked after the weak Christmas sales. Cash was coming into the company at a rate sufficient to pay its overheads, but not sufficient to pay any money to the subcontractors – who were threatening to put in winding-up petitions if they were not paid.

SUDDEN ARRIVAL AS COMPANY DOCTOR

The board of Acorn Computer Group plc comprised at this stage the two founders (Hermann Hauser, Chairman, and Christopher Curry, Managing Director), John Sutherland, Christopher Ward, and myself. We went into urgent session, together with the department heads (of finance, production, sales, and research & development) to consider what should be done to avert receivership.

One course would have been to sell the company outright to a larger firm. This we were very reluctant to do. Acorn had had a short but splendid history, and it seemed an ignominious conclusion to sell out (at a necessarily distress price) to a large company. Many of us had come to

Acorn from large companies simply because we preferred the lively and entrepreneurial spirit of the smaller company. We had no wish to return to a large one.

The other alternative was to arrange a refinancing of the company, together with an arrangement with its creditors and a cutback of overheads. This we much preferred. But it was nevertheless very painful. It was distressing to have to sack staff and shut down major projects, so soon after the company had been a model success story. It would be easier for this axe to be wielded by an outside person, such as myself, rather than by one of the founders. I accordingly volunteered to take over, on a temporary basis, as chief executive of the company, to carry out a financial and managerial reconstruction.

My offer was accepted. In early February 1985 I took temporary leave of absence from my venture capital company and moved into a spare office in the Acorn headquarters at Fulbourn Road, Cambridge, as acting chief executive.

NEW FINANCIAL ADVISERS

Our first move was to retain the merchant banking group Close Brothers as financial advisers to Acorn. This followed a recommendation by Philip Hughes, Chairman of the computer software company Logica, for whom Close Brothers acted.

A FOUR-PART PLAN

With the advice of Close Brothers, we worked out a four-part plan of action. Firstly, within the company, we would cut back expenditure severely, while doing everything possible to sustain the level of sales. Secondly, we would seek an external equity investor. Thirdly, we would negotiate revised loan arrangements from our bankers (Barclays). Fourthly, we would seek a formal arrangement with major creditors for the rescheduling of our debts. While all this went on, it would be necessary to suspend trading in the shares of Acorn.

There were two reasons why the reconstruction would have to be achieved very quickly – within 3 or 4 weeks. The first was that several creditors were already on the verge of putting in winding-up petitions, and with every week that went by there was an increasing risk that one of these (probably from a relatively small creditor) would put the company into liquidation. Secondly, with a huge question mark placed over the future of the company, sales were likely to decline rapidly. This phenomenon, sometimes referred to as the FUD factor ('fear, uncertainty and doubt'), afflicts any technology company on the brink of bankruptcy. It arises because purchasers of technology products are unlikely to buy products whose future support (and future evolution) is in doubt. With declining sales, the company would quickly run out of cash, with the likelihood of the bank putting in a receiver to protect its position.

When this four-part plan, and its urgent timetable, was first put to us by Close Brothers, it seemed frankly incredible that it could be achieved. The agreements with each of the parties would be inter-conditional, because no party would agree to bear its part of the pain if others got off lightly. Thus it would only need one party (for example, one major creditor) to refuse and the whole scheme would fall apart.

But we could see no better way forward, and therefore put our trust in the Close Brothers' plan.

THE COMPANY

My own main task during this period was to cut the company's level of expenditure by about half, while retaining within it the resources to sustain sales, and the special skills which would make the company attractive to a new equity investor.

The total staff of Acorn comprised some 450 people, organised in four functional departments: research & development, production, sales, and finance & administration. It had more than doubled in the last year, as the company had expanded rapidly into new products, markets, and countries.

Our sums showed that we would need to cut the staff to about 250 within 2 months. I decided to do this by creating a completely new organisation out of the old, and to cut the staff by picking 250 people to stay, rather than picking 200 people to go. The first organisational decision was to recast the company into four profit centres, based on Acorn's four markets: consumer, educational, business, and scientific & industrial. A managing director was picked from the senior staff of the company to head up each of these new units, and he was given a maximum head count for his business. The sum of these head counts, plus the reduced financial and administrative unit, totalled about 250.

Each of the four managing directors was asked to prepare a business plan for running his business profitably, and was given a free hand as to the mix of staff in his unit. He was then invited to claim staff at the next level immediately below him. We held a meeting to resolve, in a spirit of give and take, any cases in which the same person was bid for by more than one managing director. The process was then repeated at the next level down, and so on. Those who were not bid for were the people whom we made redundant. It was a distressing process, but by carrying out the reduction of staff in this way, we at least gave a boost to those who remained – since each was positively chosen by his boss, rather than simply escaping the axe.

There were interesting effects of this shift from functional departments meeting imposed workloads to businesses required to make a profit. Specifically, there were several cases in which the new managing directors came to me and suggested they should have less staff in certain areas; before the reorganisation they invariably pleaded for more staff to cope with the work.

A drawback of the scheme, though a stimulating one, was that several managers found themselves plunged overnight into jobs for which they had neither professional training nor practical experience. For example, only one of the four managing directors had ever managed a profit centre before. It was not difficult to find four technical directors for the four businesses, because Acorn was very rich in technical talent. But to find four marketing directors we needed to draft in people without marketing experience. The results were not ideal, and the company was later reorganised on a largely functional basis; but I think it was the most practical way of achieving a rapid shrinkage without demotivating the remaining staff.

In parallel with this reorganisation we devoted every available effort to sustaining sales and collecting cash. In a crash selling programme we mobilised dozens of staff from the technical units to act as emergency sales people – rather in the manner of the communist Chinese sending the intellectuals out into the fields. I am not sure how effective this was, but it must have helped, and it certainly demonstrated to our bankers and creditors that we were doing all we could.

OLIVETTI

Rod Kent, the managing director of Close Brothers, flew out to Ivrea in Italy to try to interest Olivetti in putting several million pounds into Acorn in return for a minority stake. He succeeded in kindling their interest, and a team flew from Ivrea to Cambridge to investigate the company – all this within 3 days of Close Brothers' appointment as Acorn's financial advisers.

Olivetti brought in their accountants, Arthur Andersen, to carry out an urgent investigation of Acorn and its business plan. Within days they had agreed in principle to participate as equity investors to the tune of about £10m, to acquire 49 per cent of Acorn. Their agreement was conditional upon the other parties, namely the bank and the major creditors, playing their part in the reconstruction.

There were four features of Acorn which attracted Olivetti. Firstly, they admired the quality of the research & development team. Secondly, they recognised Acorn's position as the European leader in educational computers, and saw this as an opportunity to establish Olivetti in educational computing worldwide. Thirdly, they liked the connection with the BBC. Fourthly, they were keen to have a presence in the Cambridge area, which they viewed as Europe's liveliest concentration of innovative computer research.

BARCLAYS

From Barclays we needed increased and confirmed banking facilities. The negotiations were rather curious, because the key factor in Barclays' mind was the attitude of Olivetti. Specifically, they needed to know whether Olivetti would come back to the aid of Acorn if more money was needed in future. These matters were sorted out directly between Barclays and Olivetti; my impression was that Olivetti gave no undertaking of this sort, but put Barclays' mind at rest by pointing out that in practice they had never allowed a company in which they had such a large stake to default on its obligations to its bank.

CREDITORS

The negotiations with the major creditors were fascinating. We owed some £12 million to the four largest, and simply did not have the money to pay. It was extremely embarrassing. The embarrassment was reduced in one case (a supplier based in Hong Kong) since we did not meet the creditor face-to-face. Instead we had the less embarrassing but equally alarming experience of dealing with a high-powered firm of City solicitors acting for him. The other creditors varied in their stance from the friendly to the abusive.

In cases where the amount of money owed to a creditor is large in relation to the creditor's business, the creditor's negotiating position is relatively weak. This is because he would cut off his own nose by putting the debtor into liquidation. Thus, although there was a lot of huffing and puffing, it was clear that the major creditors needed an amicable settlement. In fact the gravest threat in such circumstances is from a casual winding-up petition from a small creditor, who can afford to write off his debt.

After numerous strained meetings, lasting in some cases until the small hours, all five major creditors agreed to a rescheduling of their debt, with accumulated interest, over twelve monthly instalments. The negotiations were complicated by the fact that all sides wanted to take the opportunity to settle other detailed matters under dispute, such as delivery schedules, defective deliveries, and specification changes.

A BREATHING SPACE

This first reconstruction, completed in March 1985, brought in Olivetti as 49 per cent shareholder in Acorn. It enabled the company to carry on, and trading in its shares recommenced on the Unlisted Securities Market.

But worse was to come. Under the reconstruction we had undertaken to pay back to the creditors all the monies due to them, with accumulated interest, over an extended period. This required Acorn to find about £1m per month to pay its overheads (roughly halved since February) and another £1m per month to repay the historic debt to the major creditors.

This would have been possible if the micro-computer market had held up during the second quarter of 1985. But it didn't. During April and May sales were well below our expectations. This was not just an Acorn problem, it was general within the industry.

By the beginning of June it was clear that Acorn would run out of money again if it continued to pay the historic debt on its agreed schedule. There was no alternative but to suspend all payments to creditors, suspend the trading in Acorn shares, and go through the hoops of a second reconstruction.

THE SECOND RECONSTRUCTION

With the assistance of Arthur Andersen (financial advisers to Olivetti), a new reconstruction plan was devised. It depended on another £5m of equity from Olivetti. For the major creditors there was to be a write-off of half their debt (amounting to some £10m). The sweetener was that the other half (amounting likewise to about £10m) would be paid fully in cash on the date of reconstruction.

This time we were determined to put the historical problems behind us once and for all, rather than push them ahead of us. Two ingenious features of the scheme were its tax efficiency (since the creditors could reclaim VAT on the amounts written off, and could offset the remaining write-off against tax), and the fact that it did at least give the major creditors a substantial amount of cash in hand – whereas if Acorn went into receivership they would have got virtually nothing.

This time the BBC was brought in as a major creditor, and it gallantly agreed to write off about £2m owed to it by Acorn as part of the scheme.

The negotiations with the creditors were even more tense than during the previous reconstruction, partly because we were asking them to accept more pain, and partly because they had been hurt once. But eventually all agreed, with minor variations, to the plan. Barclays Bank likewise agreed to the plan, drawing some comfort from the fact that the second reconstruction would lead to Olivetti becoming 79 per cent shareholders.

THE RESCUE COMPLETED

At the end of August 1985 the second reconstruction was completed, and trading in the Acorn shares recommenced. With its historic financial problems behind it, and a new managing director (Brian Long, whom we recruited from Canada) in charge, the company was back on its feet. It has continued to prosper, and in July 1987 it was capitalised on the Unlisted Securities Market at a value of £41m.

LESSONS LEARNED

In September 1985 I left Acorn and returned to Octagon Investment Management Ltd. I had learned three important lessons: get good advisers around you, do what needs to be done even if it's unpleasant, and don't give up.

10   Scandinavian Airlines (SAS)

by Jan Carlzon, Chief Executive, SAS with Rebecca Nelson

'The only thing that counts in the new SAS is a satisfied customer.'

'We can have as many beautiful aircraft as you like and still not survive if we don't have passengers who would rather fly with SAS.'

'Make decisions so that the customer's needs are satisfied immediately.'

'SAS treats people as individuals, not as a collective. This applies to both customers and employees.'

These statements illustrate the changes in corporate culture and in goals that characterise the SAS of today. They are examples of a culture that places the customer in the centre and creates opportunities for individual initiative and commitment, that invests in market segments and backs 'winners', and believes SAS will be one of the survivors of the airline shakeout of the 1990s.

This culture has been created because it is necessary for survival in an increasingly tough market environment. The old culture was well suited to SAS before 1975, when there was a growing market with an annual passenger increase of 15–20 per cent. At that time technology, aircraft and stable operations were the main factors. Today, however, customers must believe that SAS is superior to its competitors if they are to be persuaded to fly with it rather than with another airline. Not *so* long ago, people flying from Scandinavia were instructing their travel agents *only* to book them on an SAS flight as a last resort!

The SAS CEO, Jan Carlzon, tells the story of the SAS turnaround, outlining his business and management philosophies in a people-oriented service company and even disclosing what happens when continued success becomes a company's worst enemy.

Scandinavian Airlines is the only example of a truly Scandinavian corporation, owned by Denmark, Norway and Sweden. The ownership in each country is shared equally between private interests and the governments. Consequently, when faced with problems, the CEO must find solutions that satisfy the company and all three governments. Besides that, the three countries have their own unions within SAS, which means there are forty different unions to deal with every time a major decision has to be made.

In order to put SAS's turnaround in perspective, a general view of the situation and the thinking behind the dramatic changes of the early 1980s is necessary.

The first thing we had to come to terms with was that, as a Scandinavian company, SAS was used to living in an environment where we catered largely to local consumption and sold to local markets in a marketplace with limited competition. Today we have a product sold worldwide, a requirement for global marketing and very strong international competition, all of which affects sales, whether in airline seats or SAS services.

If you run a company in a situation with limited competition and in which you sell almost everything you produce, as SAS did in the past, then it is logical to make almost all the decisions at the top. To run a company in this way the starting point has to be the company's fixed assets and its investments. The main objective is to maximise the return on the company's investments.

The method of reaching this goal is centred on protection of those investments at any cost. To do this the company must resist change, which is certainly possible, providing it is operating in a limited competitive environment.

If you want to run a successful business in a *competitive* environment, you cannot rely on investments alone. You have to shape your company to be more competitive towards your customers. This does not mean that you don't want a return on your investments; it means you will get a *better* return by having a maximised number of satisfied customers in a competitive market.

In this instance change must be encouraged at the business end, where your customers are actively engaged in their own business pursuits. To stimulate this change responsibility must be decentralised, because by encouraging people to have their own ideas, they will be able to influence their own actions for the benefit of the company.

But people have to be trained to take responsibility and to create their own authority. If a company operates in an environment with very little competition, it is obvious that revenues can be calculated in advance from year to year. You know what the revenue will be the next year, you know what will be produced, you know what the prices are going to be, allowing for inflation and so on. So the company is directed from the cost side, and the only variable is the difference between the revenue side, which is calculated in advance, and the cost side. It is a very production-oriented way of working out the company's activities, and has very little to do with what the market is really prepared to pay for.

It is possible to manage a company in this way as long as there is limited competition in the marketplace. But as soon as a competitive situation develops, the only way to run a company properly is to decide what type of customer you want and what that customer's real needs are in this market, and then to adjust your products, your services, your resources and your costs to meet the needs of the market better than your competitors.

Competition really started for the airlines with the first so-called oil crisis in 1974–5. The world market was stagnating and the market in Europe for air travel had not grown for 4 or 5 years. Oil prices were rising rapidly and there was a movement towards a more liberal policy regarding world aviation. Most of the airlines went into deficit and, as a consequence, competition rose in the market. Moreover, the competition was not always of benefit to the customers – the passengers themselves – because the airlines were not competing directly for the customers' attention. Instead, the competition adopted different methods to attract that grey market in-between: forwarders and travel agents. It became difficult for the customer to survey the situation and make the best choice.

Yesterday's situation was poor. SAS had all the negative forces which every company in a deficit situation had: declining productivity, over-capacity, and deficit operations. But worse than that was the declining service image on the ground and in the air. SAS had poor punctuality, and Copenhagen Airport, the main hub in the SAS system, was not looked upon, especially by Swedish and Norwegian customers, as a good airport, but rather as a nuisance. They tried any trick to avoid landing at Copenhagen Airport. These factors were really going to kill the company if we didn't change.

SAS had once been a first-class company, so how did its service develop such an image? Of course it had done so because for the last 5–6 years the revenue side didn't increase very much, while the cost side continued to increase automatically. It transpired that we took away services from customers with a general cost-cutting policy, only to be stuck with resources in the administration overhead, where the customers were not at all prepared to pay.

Not surprisingly, we lost market shares where we were operating. In 1975–6 SAS had some 6 per cent; in 1980–1 we had some 5.2 per cent. The share was not important; we could live with 6 per cent or 10 per cent or 3 per cent, it was only a question of adjusting the company. But we could not live with a trend that looked like this one, because it would end up on the zero line, and then the company wouldn't exist any more. In a zero-growth market SAS was giving away customers every year to other airlines which seemed to compete better for the clients during this period.

It all ended with SAS making a big deficit. From that time it was no longer possible to steer an airline from the cost side. Instead, it had to be steered from a marketing viewpoint. Having determined the markets you want to sell to, you have to develop resources to service those markets, and in order to do that, the employees must adjust the workings of the company to meet the needs of the marketplace.

That was why we selected a goal for SAS in 1981, when we were unprofitable, as were most of the European airlines at the time. We told our staff about the current state of the industry, of SAS's situation and about our goal for the future. The objective was this: to be a profitable airline in a zero-growth market. This sounds very dull, but actually it was an intellectual change for an airline. What did it mean? To say that we must achieve profitability in a zero-growth market meant that we shouldn't *calculate* ourselves to riches but that we should *work* ourselves to riches.

More interesting, we wanted to do this in airline operations itself, because very few airlines had been profitable in this sector in the past. Most airlines had achieved profitability with as small an airline operating deficit as possible while selling used aeroplanes at a high profit. We elected to do something different. We said we didn't want to be second-hand aeroplane brokers and custodians of fixed assets any more. In terms of sales we were going to be in the driver's seat. In future we would be service-oriented and get our revenues from competitive products and through specific and active marketing and selling.

So SAS went from being brokers and custodians to being a completely service-based enterprise. Everybody understands that a company being a broker of assets can be managed centrally, while a company that wants to compete in service has to pass on responsibility to people at the sharp end who are dealing daily with service and with customers.

SAS changed its emphasis. Our business strategy was to become the preferred airline for the frequent business traveller. Why did we want this? Because SAS was once formed to be the extended arm of Scandinavian business and public administration. We wanted this because it is a stable market and one with special requirements. Developing special services to meet those requirements makes it possible for SAS to establish an image in the marketplace, and this is vital in a highly competitive situation.

The concept is by no means unique. Every airline in the world knows that to be profitable you have to flirt with business travellers. But we said that, knowing this, the question was not to discover the idea but how to go about it, how to become better than the competition. The way was to put every single resource under the microscope and examine it carefully.

Our philosophy, which stands today, is that we want SAS to be 1 per cent better in 100 things rather than 100 per cent better in only one thing. We formed a new organisational structure to make it possible for us to change and adapt our services to the actual needs in the marketplace. The new structure allowed the decentralising of responsibility, giving it to the people working at the service end. The objective for the change in the organisation was to achieve flexibility in preparation for changing whatever was necessary, even if it meant changing the heaviest investments we had.

This strategy was passed on to the different profit units, or profit centres, within the organisation. Their responsibility now was to find ideas, to make decisions, and to take action to carry it out. They came back and said that to be able to do that we had to launch some 150 projects. It required an investment of approximately $40m, and an additional operating cost of approximately $12m per year. For this money, we could introduce different types of services for business travellers, both on the ground and in the air, such as EuroClass.

But more than that, we wanted to be the most punctual airline in Europe, because we knew that the first priority for a business traveller is punctuality. We wanted to send 10,000 front-line people to a service school for 2 days, and we wanted to send 2,500 middle-management people to a 3-week course in new business and management philosophies. We wanted to move sales offices from one area in one town to the business area of another, to educate our staff to be more sensitive towards the business traveller, to buy new equipment for our aeroplanes to give better service. And we did!

We agreed to run these projects and make the necessary investments. On top of our highest loss in history, before doing anything else, we added another $40m in new investments and $12m in new operating costs to get higher revenues before we earned them. This was really the unique and tough step SAS took, compared with most other airlines. But at the same time we were able to localise the kind of resources and cost factors not needed in the new business strategy – costs which never could have been identified if we had not had a clear strategy before we started to trim the organisation.

Consequently we ended up eliminating approximately $25m in costs at the same time as we accelerated spending on the new service-related investments. The point is that cutting costs in SAS's situation would have had the same effect as putting the brake on a car which is already standing still. Nothing would happen except that perhaps you would push your foot through the floor of the car and cause damage.

Meanwhile, now that we knew what kind of business we were in, and what kind of clients we wanted to attract, it was time to adjust the cost side – to cut out all the costs this special market segment was not prepared to pay for. What did we achieve by the measures we took? For one thing, after only 4 months, we became the most punctual airline. I think this is perhaps the most important result we achieved, because we knew that the highest priority for the business traveller is punctuality.

Another interesting point is how we got there. You can get people to develop their skills, not by steering them by fixed rules but by giving them total responsibility to achieve a specified result.

What *were* the other results? We turned the company around, and it was a very dramatic turnaround too. We managed to achieve a result of approximately half a billion Swedish Kronor, which is equal to $70m, in the first year, after a deficit of some $10m the year before.

Profitability as such is not the most important thing. What is most important is not that we reached this result but *how* we got there. We could have also achieved this profitability with a very centralised management and by cutting costs once again, as we had done in the past. But this profit would not have been worth very much because it would have led to a deficit position again in another 2–3 years; we would have ended up with even fewer satisfied customers and even less motivated employees.

But we did achieve the turnaround positively by investing in better services. The proof that we really managed to increase the service level came when SAS was elected the Airline of the Year by one international magazine and the best airline for business travellers by *Fortune*, the international business magazine. We increased full-fare traffic in Europe by 8 per cent, and full-fare traffic on intercontinental routes by 16 per cent in a zero-growth market. We managed to reduce our overheads by 25 per cent, i.e. every fourth dollar in our administrational overheads, because we figured that these were costs for which our clients, the business travellers, were not prepared to pay. Meanwhile we figured out that we did not need that much administration or overhead resources now, since we had passed responsibility to people within the organisation.

Investment in long-term strengths meant a durable profit that would grow in future years. Satisfied customers also meant satisfied and motivated staff. That is the real resource, the real asset for the future of SAS. In the airline business you find the asset side of the balance sheet is still written in terms of so many aircraft at a value of so many billion dollars. But the real value and test of an airline is how many satisfied customers, and how many satisfied employees, did it end up with during the year. These are the ingredients the airline needs for the future: the customer who is prepared to fly again with the airline next year and the employee who is prepared to perform just as well next year. The *way* we made the profit is as important to us as is the money we actually earned.

So what had we really done in the company? We had begun to realise for the first time that there is only one source prepared to contribute to SAS's running costs, and that is the airline's customers. If we wanted customers to pay our costs, we had to listen to their demands. In return we have to give service which really satisfies the needs of the marketplace. Since people working in the front line are those who know customer demands best, they are the ones who should shape the service we at SAS give.

Then we queried our own roles, those of us who work in administration, in technical development and so on. Our role is to listen to the demands from our front-line people. What do they need to be able to provide the services the market requests? The front-line staff have to be able to stick up for the customers and give them the service they demand. We vowed that the situation should never again be the other way around, as it is in companies where the support team is called the administration, which instructs the front line what to do for the customers, whether they want it or not. This behaviour is only possible as long as there is no competition in the market, and as long as the market is increasing. But it can never work in a competitive situation, not if you want to survive and develop your business.

Within SAS we said the front line would make the decisions from now on, and not the other way around. That is what we call being a market-oriented company. We collected the views most commonly expressed in the company during the first year. We found out that the most important thing for a person, whether employee or customer, was to know that he or she was really needed. We found that a person who was no longer restricted by instructions, orders or policies felt a sense of release when given responsibility through training and information. Finally we laid it down that an individual *without* information could not take responsibility. An individual who *has* information cannot avoid taking responsibility. That is why a manager has to educate and inform his staff.

We used to think of SAS as a fleet of aircraft, a technical overhaul plant, or an administration building somewhere in Scandinavia. But our new attitude helped us discover that SAS was really not much more than the contact between one customer and one SAS employee working in the front line. When these two people met, SAS appeared, and that was our 'moment of truth'. The perception of SAS was based on the individual contact between one customer and several SAS employees working in the front line who met as the customer was processed through our chain of services.

SAS had 12 million customers in 1986. All of them wanted to be treated as individuals. If each of these customers met five SAS employees working in the front line, that means that SAS appeared 60 million times in 1986. We have calculated that every such meeting between an individual customer and an individual SAS employee lasts about 15 seconds. Everybody understands that if we honestly want to listen to the individual demand from the business traveller and give in return the service he or she deserves, we have to act within these 15 seconds. Otherwise we are out of business.

That is why we can no longer steer the company from a centralised administration where we issue policies, instructions and orders that cover 60 million occasions, with every occasion lasting for 15 seconds, and still kid ourselves that we can give an individualised service to our target market, the business traveller. The only way to do it is to ensure that we have employees who are so familiar with the objective and strategies of the company that they can exercise their own responsibility and act within these 15 seconds. Not only do they have the responsibility, they also have the authority to act within this brief time.

After 1 year SAS had reached its goal, and airline operations were profitable. After 2 years we had fulfilled our objective by winning awards for being the best airline in the world. We were credited in magazines as having the best service for the business traveller.

Suddenly a new situation developed in the organisation. It was no longer clear to everybody what the company's new goal should be. You could see in this situation how different groups of people in the company started to act on their own. Every group set its own objectives, which were often related to its own performance or task. Instead of people trying to improve themselves in their work, they started to compete with each other in the company, and set different goals for different groups. The large numbers of skilled technicians, pilots and all those people who had been used to looking upon themselves as the centre of everything felt threatened by the stress on service orientation. They had to be reminded that the best service is to get the customer down on the ground safely and therefore their expertise was paramount.

What is the role of a leader in a decentralised organisation in such a situation? The only option is to assume a strategic leadership. That means you have to find a new goal and form new strategies which are logical to the majority of the people in the organisation.

It transpired that most of the employees were fearful of what might happen if a more liberal climate developed in the airline market. If free competition developed in Scandinavia, could the new SAS survive? Could SAS still compete? The reason for this fear was that steps had been taken by governments in the Common Market towards liberalising the airline industry.

The fear was analysed and countered with the only goal which would really unite the staff and win a new alignment. We decided that SAS should survive, but also expand in a climate of free competition. In other words SAS had better prepare itself to be competitive in a free-market environment. If we didn't, we would have all the problems the US airlines have had. Survival meant being better prepared than our competitors the day liberalisation came to Europe, because everybody realises it will happen sooner or later. Being prepared for survival and expansion in the midst of new competition – that is the new goal of SAS.

The only way to meet the competition, survive and also expand is to be so efficient and so excellent in everything you do that you can beat every company cutting prices or any one competing in quality. We wanted to combine these two opportunities in SAS. We wanted to continue to be both efficient and excellent, for it would be pointless to concentrate on one to the detriment of the other. SAS has set standards which everybody knows and respects. Safety, technical standards and service are the pillars SAS was built on and they remain our pillars for the future. The most important factor which will decide whether SAS will continue to be competitive or not is how the people of SAS act in relation to our standards and how prepared they are to improve the company's efficiency and good name by their own performance.

In SAS we are now trying to work out an organisation with three different levels. The first is a strategic management level, whose responsibility is to adapt the company to future threats and opportunities and formulate objectives to guide the company into the future. The next level deals with resource planning, and taking responsibility for results. The third level includes the people who conduct the business at hand, with responsibility and authority to carry out their own ideas, make their own decisions and act on their own.

The first two are leadership levels and the third is the level that includes the middle-management bosses. In SAS today these bosses are not making every decision. The bosses are all the people who take care of the service and the products, and they all have the responsibility and authority to make their own decisions.

As the enlightened companies must take account of the changes in society, so too must the unions. The union's function today is to play an increasing role in the entire process as an ally and not as a group in conflict with top management.

SAS has been described as one of the best turnaround experiences to date. In fact American management guru Tom Peters once said, 'I could give you five different reasons why it *should* be impossible to change SAS. But they did it anyway, in record time. SAS has given managements just what they've been looking for: a ray of hope.'

by Don McCrickard, Managing Director,
TSB COMMERCIAL HOLDINGS LTD

United Dominions Trust is a well known, large finance house – true or false? Only partly true, as UDT has been much more than that for many years.

In 1986 UDT Holdings Ltd changed its name to TSB Commercial Holdings Ltd, its trading activities being structured into a group of four lending businesses under United Dominions Trust Ltd, the old finance house, and a group of three motor-related businesses under Swan National Ltd. Let's look at this in more detail.

ACTIVITIES AND STRUCTURE

UDT's Sales Finance Division provides retail-motor and home-improvement finance for the public through dealers, as well as fleet finance for major operators. This represents the long-standing traditional credit business of UDT, and is still our largest lending activity, with more than £880m being employed. The UDT Consumer Finance Division lends to the private consumer direct, or through intermediaries, carrying on a new and growing business of mortgage and personal finance. The UDT Corporate Loans Division, a long established and substantial business, offers big ticket finance for medium and large companies.

These three businesses, although operating independently, are divisions of United Dominions Trust Ltd, which also owns UDT Bank Ltd in the Irish Republic.

[125]

United Dominions Trust Ltd is a subsidiary of TSB Commercial Holdings Ltd, as is Swan National Ltd, to which we shall return later. The structure of the TSB Commercial Holdings Group (a direct subsidiary of the TSB Group plc) is shown in Figure 11.1.

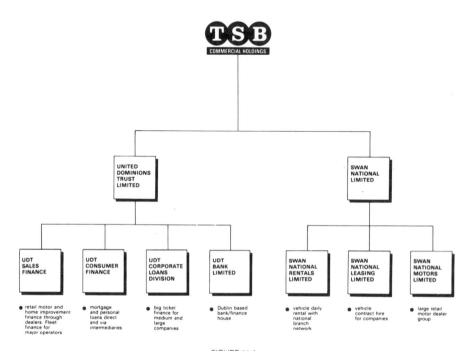

FIGURE 11.1

While looking at this structure, it may be helpful to note the size and growth of the total businesses during the last 5 years, expressed in Table 11.1 in terms of return on average funds employed. The relative contributions from the finance house services (UDT) and the vehicle rental, leasing and distribution activities (Swan National) can be seen from the Table 11.2.

It will be evident from Table 11.2 that the underlying improvement in financial performance has been impressive, with a quadrupling of pre-tax profits from £7.6m to £31.4m in evidence over the period 1983–87.

As we shall see, the group structure is new, introduced as a key element in our recovery. The pre-1984 structure had not been the result of conscious design but rather the product of history and banking law, and more recently had comprised the residual elements of rationalisation resulting from the secondary banking crisis of the mid-1970s.

TABLE 11.1

	Average funds (£m)	Profit (£m)	Return on funds (%)
1983	919	7.6	0.83
1984	1,049	10.4	0.99
1985	1,167	13.8	1.18
1986	1,314	17.4	1.32
1987	1,427	31.4	2.20

TABLE 11.2

Operating profits (£m)	1983	1984	1985	1986	1987
Finance-house services	6.1	5.6	10.1	14.3	24.5
Vehicle rental, leasing and distribution	4.4	4.9	7.5	7.4	9.7
	10.5	10.5	17.6	21.7	34.2

Note: Profits are before loan stock interest, group development and central expenses.

HISTORY OF UDT

The history of United Dominions Trust is germane to its recent problems. It began in 1919 when an attempt by an American bank to open a London branch faltered in the face of stiff competition. The young Scots manager, John Gibson Jarvie, had to find something different, and by a prime example of lateral thinking came to invent the Consumer Finance

House industry. The business of personal credit prospered hand in hand with the growth of the ownership of motor cars – ideal items for retail finance – and received the seal of respectability in 1930 when the Bank of England demonstrated its approval by taking shares in UDT.

By 1974 UDT, still acknowledged as Europe's largest finance house, had in fact developed into one of Britain's best known companies, as a diverse conglomerate group trading on a worldwide basis, and its stock was a favoured blue chip. The group's balance sheet assets then totalled £1,255m (equivalent to £4,556m in 1987 terms). The original finance house, United Dominions Trust Ltd, was also the holding company of this large group, resulting in an awkward structure which it would have been difficult and expensive to alter while UDT remained both a public company and, under the law of that period, a bank. The wide variety of worldwide activities carried on by the UDT group before 1974 ranged, for example, from merchant banking to precision engineering, and from commodity futures contracts to motor dealerships.

The causes and results of the secondary banking crisis of 1974 are today well known. When depositors withdrew their funds from finance houses – the problem being exacerbated for UDT by its worldwide spread – the Bank of England organised the provision of support funds through the 'lifeboat'. This clearly implied that finance houses could no longer continue as independent organisations but needed parents with ample funding capability. While its competitors quickly found shelter, UDT was then too large to be easily digested, and consequently spent the late 1970s in the task of divesting itself of activities other than those still carried on today by TSB Commercial Holdings Ltd, as shown in Figure 11.1.

TSB TAKES OVER

By 1980 UDT had finally repaid the 'lifeboat' support funds and had become slim enough to attract takeover interests, and in 1981 it was acquired by the Trustee Savings Bank Group. Even then its management continued for a while to be still occupied with residual overseas problems, so that, after a period of assimilation into the TSB Group, it was in late 1983 that work on the turnaround of the remaining businesses in the

UK and Ireland began in earnest. When I arrived on the scene from American Express as the newly appointed Managing Director, my brief from TSB Group Chairman Sir John Read was to (a) return UDT Holdings to acceptable financial health and (b) prepare the business to play its part within the TSB Group following flotation.

On taking stock of the situation, I found that the motor businesses were performing much better than the lending businesses, and it was upon the latter that I decided to concentrate my initial attention.

STRENGTHS AND WEAKNESSES

Examining UDT's lending activities, I found a number of strengths and a long list of weaknesses. The strengths included a deep reservoir of staff experience in the complex business of finance-house lending, although a number of senior managers had been promoted into other jobs elsewhere in the TSB Group. Indeed this brain drain was to continue for some time – not surprisingly, as the TSB Group was itself reorganising and had originally perceived the high quality of some of UDT's senior managers to be one of the attractions of the acquisition. I also found an excellent state of industrial relations, a welcome find in view of the obvious need for reorganisation and change. Most importantly for a financial institution, the reputation of UDT had remained remarkably intact, as witness its success in replacing 'lifeboat' funds with deposits through its natural funding markets. There were other strengths, but the problems and weaknesses seemed formidable.

To produce now a long Mikado-like list of the problems confronting UDT's lending businesses at that time would be as pointless as it would be tedious. Instead I will simply note a random selection, some of which were operational in character, others raising issues of long-term strategy.

- *Corporate structure.* With the holding company being also the main trading company, the true profitability of the several businesses was unclear. In addition, this structure starved newly emerging lines of business of the resources needed to ensure take-off.

- *Accountability*. There was no clear-cut profit accountability for any part of the group's business below my own level.

- *Management organisation*. The business was organised around the directorate rather than around the needs of the business and the marketplace.

- *Business strategy*. There was no clear agreement on where UDT was going nor how it would get there. The budget was mistakenly regarded as a plan.

- *Technology*. Lack of strategy and of funds had left UDT with worn-out systems and technologically behind its competitors.

- *Overhead costs*. These were far too high for the business, largely as a result of overmanning.

- *Remuneration*. Salary and benefits levels were well behind TSB and other finance-house standards. The morale of managers and staff was low.

- *Overdues*. The main-stream instalment credit business suffered various unaddressed weaknesses, a particularly serious one being the high proportion of borrowers in default.

The list could continue. The bottom line result of this was that in 1982 the UK finance-house activities were losing money.

FIRST STEPS TO RECOVERY

The first task was to differentiate between those activities where remedial action was needed as a matter of urgency and those which would need further analysis as their solutions would have a longer-term effect on our business strategy. Early in 1984 action began on several fronts simultaneously, rapidly gathering momentum as morale improved when managers and staff perceived that a determined effort was being made to find a cure.

Eighteen months later, by June 1985, it was clear that significant progress had been made. We had, for example, achieved the following:

- The businesses of the TSB Commercial Holdings Group (as it is now called) had been reorganised into seven independent and accountable profit centres to reflect their separate identities and operating characteristics properly. (The acquisition of invoice discounting and factoring company Boston Financial Ltd in June 1987, now renamed UDT Commercial Finance, gives TSB Commercial Holdings its eighth subsidiary.)

- A Head Office relocation from central London to north London had been completed, yielding annual rent and rates savings of £1.1m.

- Retirements, early retirements and other house-cleaning measures had paved the way for a substantial change in people and attitudes. Four external general manager level appointments had been made.

- A number of other key management appointments had been made to introduce fresh blood, new ideas and a much needed sense of urgency.

- A structured business planning system had been developed and integrated within the TSB Group system.

- An appropriate mid-term operating strategy had been defined for each of our businesses where none had previously existed.

- A major expense reduction programme to tackle UDT's unwieldy overhead problem had been completed, and manning levels within the UK finance businesses had been significantly reduced. These, and other related measures, had brought annual savings of nearly £5m.

- Progress had been made in closing the salary gap between UDT and its major competitors.

- Good relations with the Banking Insurance and Finance Union had been successfully sustained during the difficult and disruptive period of reorganisation.

- A major investment to automate our outdated manual debt collection system had been made and this had been augmented by establishing a field collection force to collect early overdues. Benefits from both were beginning to flow.

- Another large investment had been committed to credit scoring in order to improve the quality of loan underwriting. UDT had also been responsible for developing this technology for TSB Group banks and operating companies.

- Preliminary investments had been made in three other important areas where UDT lagged behind, namely branch automation, management information systems and the 18-year-old instalment credit system. The payback would come eventually from lower unit costs and increased competitiveness.

- All UDT's overseas residual assets (except in the Republic of Ireland) had been disposed of and the proceeds had been repatriated.

Naturally some of these changes had been achieved early in this 18-month period. One of the first was the expense reduction programme, where we adopted a zero-based analysis approach to the cost of our central service functions, such as accounts, personnel, administration, computer and management services, and our large debt collection activity, then still centralised. This significantly reduced the cost of these central services and improved effectiveness. We then went on to decentralise many of them by making them the line responsibility of the businesses they serviced. This increased the accountability of the line managers, and also increased the flexibility to respond to the needs of the TSB Group should it ever wish to change the shape of TSB Commercial Holdings Ltd.

Meanwhile, again early in this same period, the operational problems deep within the business itself were being energetically tackled by keen new senior managers, supported by longer established colleagues whose enthusiasm had now been rejuvenated. This blend of new ideas and long experience proved invaluable in maintaining stability while improving what is, after all, a risk business, and became an important element in improving staff morale and in maintaining excellent industrial relations during a difficult period of reorganisation and change.

THE SECOND PHASE

So what of the 3 years that have now passed since June 1985?

This has been a period when the restructured businesses have redirected their strategies and improved their profitability. For example, the bad-debt problem of 4 years ago had long been one of our heaviest millstones, and had reached chronic proportions. By the end of 1986 the bad-debt ratio was well down, showing greater and more consistent improvement than the finance industry average – and there is every prospect of a further reduction.

The heavy investment in technology, begun 3 years ago in order to make up for our 'lost years', is progressing well and is already resulting in improved decision-making, lower unit costs and better operational control. In addition, we have continued to keep a firm grip on overhead costs, so that manning levels and operating expense ratios in the established lending businesses have been greatly reduced, with significantly higher business volumes being supported by a headcount no higher than 4 years ago. (Indeed, taking into account the whole of TSB Commercial Holdings Ltd, profit per employee increased from £1,847 in 1983 to £7,285 in 1987.)

Most importantly, new lines of business have been established. UDT Sales Finance has aggressively developed a car fleet and leasing business, while UDT Consumer Finance has penetrated into the profitable market for larger balance first mortgages – to give but two examples. Various cross-selling activities also have been engaged with other parts of the TSB Group.

A HINDSIGHT VIEW

I recently asked a long-serving UDT executive whether, with the hindsight of the last 4 years, he considered any one of these measures as having been pre-eminently influential in our turnaround. His reply was interesting. He said he considered all had been necessary to deal with our range of difficulties but that, with the longer view in mind, he believed the pivotal decision to have been the restructuring of the UDT finance-house activity into independent businesses. This had, he felt, immediately been perceived by managers and staff as conveying an important message about our future and had restored confidence. The advantages this reorganisation produced were:

- Management profit accountability.

- Increased staff identification with business objectives and hence greater enthusiasm and a feeling of 'ownership'.

- Flexibility for future organisational development as a result of having put a modular structure into place.

- An improved ability to move into new markets with great speed.

My colleague considers this last point vital, as the reorganisation, in creating the new Consumer Finance Division, offered a real opportunity to move into the direct loans business as a parallel activity to UDT's established Sales Finance and Corporate Lending. He recalls that this market had been previously neglected, because it had been regarded not as a separate business but merely as a bolt-on extra to the existing business. So the management had not then taken it seriously and did not have the specialised knowledge it demanded. That had been changed by establishing it as a separate, accountable business with clear objectives and an agreed business plan. The fact that this had grown to a £700m business by the end of 1987 is testimony to the wisdom of the decision.

The interesting point this executive makes is that this development had given instant encouragement to managers and staff and to our union organisers, many of whom had been critical of the company's neglect of this potential new market. Immediately it was perceived that the company was now seriously planning a long-term future; the traumas of cost reduction and reorganisation became acceptable as a necessary means to a worthwhile end instead of being just another unpalatable twist in an all too familiar downward spiral. So attitudes had changed and morale improved.

UDT BANK

I have said little about our subsidiary in the Irish Republic, UDT Bank Ltd. Based in Dublin with branches in other parts of Ireland, it has suffered from a difficult economy and has encountered problems similar to those experienced by UDT in Britain. Suffice it to say that the business is beginning to respond to remedies now seen to be effective in other parts of our group. In particular, staff morale has been invigorated by new top management and the company is winning the battle against overdues and bad debts.

So, standing back and taking a view of our leading activities today, I believe that the corner has been well and truly turned. But there is still a great deal of potential to be unlocked and this will show itself in improved profitability.

SWAN NATIONAL

How during these 4 years have the businesses of Swan National Ltd progressed? As Table 11.2 shows, they have made a steady and improving contribution to the operating profits of TSB Commercial Holdings Ltd, and their profitability is impressive.

Today Swan National Motors Ltd (formerly Valkyrie Motor Holdings Ltd), comprising sixteen dealerships, is among Britain's largest twenty motor dealer groups. Its origin, in view of the theme of this chapter, is interesting. In the 1960s the group consisted of an intensive care unit into which UDT took defaulting motor traders to convert them back to profitability and sell as a means of protecting loans otherwise irrecoverable. But the expert management brought in for that purpose proved so successful that UDT adopted the strategy of retaining motor dealerships permanently within the group.

Swan National Rentals and Swan National Leasing Ltd, both today strongly established in their markets, also grew out of a small business which 25 years ago featured as a UDT bad debt.

Now, if we consider the motor finance activities of UDT together with the sales activities of Swan National, it is a fact that TSB Commercial Holdings Ltd last year either financed, sold, leased or held available for rent a total of 350,000 vehicles, giving it a major and influential position with the UK motor industry.

IN CONCLUSION

It will be evident that the turnaround of the old UDT Holdings, which commenced at the end of 1983, has been an outstanding success. Profits have quadrupled, return on assets nearly tripled and the head count held at its 1983 level.

I believe that the newly constituted TSB Commercial Holdings Group is today highly motivated by what it has achieved and it now has an impressive breadth and depth of commercial managements across its eight operating companies. I believe we are well positioned to make an important contribution to the TSB Group's dynamic future.

12 Italtel

*by Marisa Bellisario, Managing Director
and Chief Executive Officer*, ITALTEL

The Italtel corporate story in the last 6 years has been defined by observers as a case study in a company turnaround. Since 1981 in fact, Italtel, the largest Italian manufacturing company in the telecommunications industry, has gone through a remarkable strategic, structural and even cultural change, leading to corporate recovery and to the company's launch on the international arena.

In early 1981 Italtel had the necessary resources and know-how to reassert its leading position in Italian telecommunications, but was constrained by a financial and organisational situation on the verge of collapse. The corporate structure was overgrown and sliding towards inefficiency. Company losses were huge, reaching 10 million lire per employee; the operating loss amounted to 200 billion lire, net sales to 500 billion lire and financial liabilities to 700 billion lire; the value of inventories was almost equal to revenues.

Moreover corporate culture was based on the myth of the traditional 'good electromechanical product' manufactured in large factories by a mostly blue-collar workforce. Little concern was given to competitiveness in terms of costs and features. This approach was a severe constraint at a time in which rapid product and market changes were taking place in world telecommunications with the shift from electromechanical to electronic technologies.

In company laboratories researchers, despite their considerable technological capabilities, were unable to transform the first Italian electronic switching prototype, the Proteo, into a successful product. The project had begun in 1965 and was being carried out in total isolation from corporate activities and the external environment. The prevalent feeling among researchers was that resources were unlimited and research could be pursued *per se*, for pure scientific pleasure, with no concern for production requirements. Accordingly the project of a second-generation Proteo exchange had also started with a small group in the USA. How and when these exchanges would be produced, with what resources and what facilities, were unresolved issues.

To recover from such a situation, Italtel chose an innovation-oriented strategy, based on a sharp boost in productivity and efficiency and the rapid introduction of electronic technologies. Its implementation was supported by Italtel's shareholders, IRI and Stet, with capital injections covering the losses incurred in the late 1970s and early 1980s. Moreover a series of strategic actions defined by Italtel's new managerial team allowed the company to return to profit by 1983 and, since then, to fully finance itself through its positive cash flow without additional funding. Corporate recovery coincided with the company's technological transformation to electronics, which is now successfully nearing completion.

First, Italtel's monolithic and rigid structure was changed by forming into a group of companies that each operated in a specific market and product segment. Italtel was thus put in a position to handle the full spectrum of communications, from public telecommunications to office automation, and to satisfy customer requests with a systematic approach, whereby different Italtel subsidiaries worked together to implement a turnkey project.

Second, highly motivated human resources were injected into the company to regenerate managerial and professional ranks. In early 1981 a new top management team with a more market- and research-oriented culture than its predecessor was assembled. In fact about two-thirds of the current 320 executives were appointed from outside the company or joined it after 1981. An MBO (Management by Objectives) system was introduced to promote their personal commitment towards the achievement of specific objectives. Since 1983 moreover a reservoir of future executives has been formed by hiring young university graduates, and mainly assigning them to research and development activities. In the 1983–6 period about 1,000 graduates were hired, 360 of them joining the company in 1986.

Because of the technological shift, this recruitment policy was necessarily coupled with a reduction through redundant workers, mainly blue collars. The company's management explained to the unions that sacrifices in terms of employment were necessary for corporate survival and, with union agreement, reduction was achieved through non-traumatic measures (incentives to leave, early retirement, voluntary transfers). Personnel was thus reduced from 30,000 people in 1980 to 17,700 at the end of 1986. A stable level of about 16,000 employees is expected by year-end 1989.

In 1981 the only alternative to this solution would have been to close down. This would have meant not only higher social costs in terms of unemployment but also the loss of the company's accrued experience and know-how, thereby giving up all possibility of maintaining Italy's autonomous technological expertise in telecommunications.

Part of the redundant labour force resulting from technological changes at Italtel has also been absorbed through a new form of labour contract introduced in 1986 and called *contratto di solidarietà* or 'solidarity contract'. It has been recently implemented in Italy by legislation, and a similar scheme is being carried out in France. By the terms of these contracts, which currently concern about 80 per cent of employees, the working schedule has been reduced to 35 hours a week, and the cost of the 5 non-worked hours is borne by Social Security as well as by the workers, whose salaries are proportionally reduced.

Third, to prepare personnel for the new skills and responsibilities required in the Electronics Age, a massive in-house training programme for employees at all levels was launched. Training was also a basic tool for developing a corporate culture based on a positive approach to change. Today electronics accounts for over 80 per cent of production (against 20 per cent in 1980) and this transformation was achieved by using mostly 'retrained' personnel.

Fourth, research and development management was directed towards market requirements. Italtel R&D laboratories worked more closely than before with production and marketing. Programming and responsibilities were clearly defined, making co-operation between research and the various other corporate functions the norm. Research activity on second-generation digital public switching systems was brought under clear timetables, budgets and controls. The system prototypes were thus transformed into a full range of digital public exchanges called Linea UT; large-scale production began in 1984.

Italtel's R&D commitment is reflected by the level of investment in this field, which reached 152 billion lire in 1986, equivalent to 11.5 per cent of sales. This percentage is in line with that of the most innovative American and Japanese companies. Staff numbering 2,350 are presently employed in R&D at Italtel, using the most advanced CAD tools. A communication and data-processing network, with over 100 workstations and more than 800 terminals, connects Italtel facilities throughout Italy, ensuring co-ordination between design, development, production and sales activities.

The main result of this innovation-oriented approach is the full renewal of Italtel's product range. The successful launch of the Linea UT digital public switching systems (today 700 UT exchanges are installed in Italy) is being confirmed by an increase in sales and new contracts in foreign markets. The Linea UT system range is being extended to large-capacity applications: the Linea UT module, connecting up to 100,000 users, is scheduled to enter service in this year. New product lines have been introduced also in transmission, notably fibre optic equipment. These systems, together with developments in the switching sector, will represent the basic infrastructure for the future wide-band integrated services digital network (ISDN), transmitting all types of information – voice, data, texts and images in motion. Moreover, in private telecommunications, Italtel has introduced more than forty new end-user products since 1982, and has successfully entered the very competitive office automation market.

Finally, Italtel's activity is diversifying to new areas and sectors in which existing resources can be channelled to strengthen the company's development further. A new company, Italtel Telesis, was created in 1985 to develop telematic applications in the fields of environmental monitoring, traffic automation and control, building automation and in other non-traditional uses of telecommunications. The most recent new subsidiary, Italtel Tecnoelettronica, established in 1986, marks the company's entry into the European electronics components market with the know-how and technologies acquired from producing components for telecom systems.

Italtel's recovery programme has been supported by an external and internal relations approach based on maximum transparency in corporate communications. The company's concern has been to explain to all – employees, customers, unions, government and public opinion – where it is heading and what rationale underlies its strategies. To this effect, relations with the media were emphasised, together with the widespread distribution of written information. A 'transparency' policy is also applied in relations with the unions, which are called to participate in the decision-making process regarding major organisational issues and are systematically informed about corporate strategic plans. This policy helped to gradually build a general consensus towards the company's turnaround. The aim was to inform people that not only Italtel's survival was at stake, but also the prospect of an autonomous Italian telecommunications industry.

The positive effects of these actions are reflected by Italtel's most recent economic and financial results: 1986 was the fourth consecutive year the company recorded a profit – 75 billion lire after taxes (up to 80 per cent over 1985). Consolidated sales reached 1,315 billion lire and per capita sales amounted to 84.8 million lire (respectively up 7 per cent and 24 per cent over 1985). These figures are an indication of the company's renewed economic and technological strength. Today Italtel is in a position to compete effectively and autonomously in a rapidly evolving market and to take up the challenges of telecommunications in the 1990s.

13 Tesco

by Ian MacLaurin, Chairman, TESCO

Little more than a decade ago, Tesco was close to being written off by the markets, a situation due, in part, to a sense of complacency induced by its former achievements. Then morale in the company was falling almost as fast as its City rating and its market share – and it was a favourite pastime among analysts to compare its 'time of troubles' with their favoured stock, Sainsbury.

Now, more than a decade later, a commentator in one of the industry's leading trade journals, *Retail and Distribution Management*, posed the question: 'Will the enormously confident Sainsbury be overtaken by the newly revitalised Tesco, given the operational gearing of the latter?' As Chairman of Tesco, I can tell you that only one thing is certain: my own company will not fall victim a second time to history's trap. We know now that nothing fails like success.

Tesco operates in the most competitive sector of the UK economy, and one in which success is not only notoriously elusive but also notoriously short-lived for those who believe they have found the secret of its durability. Obviously the idea of easy continuing success is absurd, not least when change has moved into the fast lane, overtaking the time we have to adjust to it.

It's a truth that may be intimidating, but it is one that Tesco has had to come to terms with these past 10 years. Until the late 1960s the seemingly inexorable growth of the company (in 1945 a London and Home Counties multiple operating out of little more than 100 stores: by 1970 a national group operating from 735 shops) had tended to disguise the paradoxical link between success and its *doppelganger*, failure. For a quarter of a century the company had sustained an unbroken pattern of growth in turnover, in market share, in profits.

The very speed and magnitude of the Company's expansion, however, had disguised certain fundamental problems within the company. The very name Tesco was regarded as a talisman, and the nature of its success self-perpetuating. The company became careless of the fact that conditions were changing around it. While Tesco reflected on its achievements in the immediate past, the competition reflected on ways to curb its success in the future.

Cracks in Tesco's façade were soon to be exposed. By the mid-1970s Tesco shares were selling at around 20p, and brokers were near-unanimous in their advice to 'sell' Tesco stock. The company's share of the growth market was static and its development programme had come to a virtual halt.

For the independent observer the question may well have been whether Tesco would survive as a free-standing entity or, whether, with the continuing rationalisation of the industry, it would fall victim to a merger or takeover – moves at which, until comparatively recently, the company itself had been so adept. The answer to such a question is simple. Without radical changes in the philosophy of the company, without its seeing beyond the comfortable illusion of success to the very real possibility of failure, and without a major transformation of the entire character of the company, there would have been no Tesco.

Today this is easily said. Ten years ago it was a problem of vast proportions. What in practice could be done to reposition the company, and recover its former trading momentum? How was it possible to restore market confidence in 'the ailing giant of the High Street', as one headline termed it in 1974?

Bertrand Russell never tired of remarking that, given the right questions, anyone can obtain the right answers. The dictum applied exactly to Tesco's situation. The first need was to determine precisely what *were* the problems within the company, before deciding what could be done to resolve them. The immediate problems were perceived as twofold. On the one hand the company was trading with an image which had been successful in the 1950s and 1960s, but had rapidly diminishing relevance to the 1970s. On the other, due to the weakness of its development programme, Tesco operated in small and often inadequate units which reinforced the impression that the company had lost touch with market reality.

Underlying both problems of course were management attitudes based on the conviction that what had served so well in the past would serve equally well in the future. All the evidence might contradict the assumption but it remained an article of faith that was ultimately tested to breaking point over the issue of trading stamps.

Throughout the 1960s Tesco had been a major exponent of stamps, and during that decade the Green Shield emblem had become virtually synonymous with the company's identity. By the mid-1970s, however, there were growing doubts not only about the value of the Tesco's annual investment in stamping but also about their impact on the customer's perception of the company. It could be argued that trading stamps, and all they represented, were symptomatic not so much of the traditional Tesco as of the traditional attitudes that dominated Tesco management.

As long as those attitudes prevailed, stamping would remain a part of Tesco – with all that this implied for the future of the company. The issue finally came to a head in the spring of 1977, when, by a single vote, it was agreed to drop stamps. Three months later, on the day following the Silver Jubilee celebrations of the accession of Queen Elizabeth II, the company announced the decision – allied to a massive price-cutting campaign thanks to the economies achieved by abandoning stamps.

The story of the day that Tesco dropped Green Shield is now a part of marketing folklore: within just 6 months the company doubled its market share, and its turnover rose by more than 100 per cent. There could be no denying the quick success of the decision to abandon stamps, though subsequently it has tended to mask the altogether more important fact that the success of Operation Checkout (as the dropping of stamps was termed) effectively marked a clean break with the past as far as Tesco was concerned.

Almost half a century has passed since Sir John Cohen had first established the company as one retailer among the multiple pack of the 1930s, and while no one could gainsay his achievements, Checkout effectively symbolised the first stage in a radical shift in the entire trading strategy of the company. However, while it takes time to formulate a new corporate strategy, the runaway success of Checkout created an immediate demand for the re-evaluation of Tesco's store and development programme.

If the company was already aware of inadequacies in its stores, Checkout forcibly confirmed the need to do something about them. Many traditional units were totally incapable of handling the new business generated post-June 1977, whilst in the same year Tesco's development budget totalled little more than £6m – or less than half the cost, at present prices, of opening one new store. The problem was clear: unless the company could accelerate its development programme while reducing the number of its smaller units, the mid-term gains resulting from Checkout would be at risk.

Tesco had been among the pioneers of supermarketing in the 1950s, but it was slow to recognise the potential of new, even larger stores being developed by the competition. The hypermarket or superstore – a US innovation – was gaining increasing favour on the Continent by the 1960s. Such units cater largely for car-borne shoppers and are based on edge-of-town or out-of-town sites.

It was only in 1975, and well behind such groups as Carrefour and Asda, that Tesco opened its first large store at Irlam, on the outskirts of Manchester. The priority, and a critical one, was to make up lost ground on the competition – and within 2 years of launching Checkout, the Company's development budget had grown twelvefold, against a background of continuing reduction in the number of smaller trading units. Thus by 1980 the company was operating out of only 550 stores – yet its trading area had grown by 300,000 square feet.

But it was not only that this new generation of stores allowed Tesco to keep pace with the competition. Equally important, they provided the company with the means for transforming its trading identity. Indeed, if the new identity of the company first test-marketed at the launch of Checkout had not been complemented by the development of attractive modern stores, a damaging conflict of image would have arisen – our High Street identity contrasting vividly with the whole thrust of our new marketing programme.

By the late 1970s there was a growing resolution between the two elements within this equation, as the consistent increase in the company's turnover indicated – from £953m in 1978 to £1,201m in 1979, rising again to £1,530m in 1980. Inevitably the near-explosive growth, both in the volume of Tesco business and in the size of Tesco stores, created problems of their own – as much in the demand for new management skills as for new management systems.

In the early days of the company it's said that Sir John Cohen could balance Tesco's profit and loss account on the back of an envelope. Much had already changed in the company's first half-century but Checkout, and all that followed, demanded an acceleration in the pace of change, for there is a quantum difference between running a supermarket of 9,000 or 10,000 square feet with a staff of twenty supporting a six-figure annual turnover, and a store of six, eight, or even ten times this size – a difference as much in management attitudes as in the stock control, marketing, merchandising and personnel systems, all of which have to achieve a new degree of sophistication.

Since the 1960s Tesco had been running a small training unit. By the late 1970s that unit was undergoing rapid expansion in order to develop the essential in-house skills needed not only to handle the new business being generated by the company but also to maintain a high level of service in the growing number of large stores becoming operational. Since time immemorial retailing has been a people business, but in the post-war years there has always been the danger that the growing application of economies of scale to the business would tend to dehumanise the shopper, more especially when allied to the introduction of advanced systems.

Although these two developments occurred in isolation, it is arguable that the first, the growth of new superstores, would have been virtually unmanageable without the second, new technology. A modern Tesco unit trades in as many as 18,000 lines, turning over upwards of £1m a week. It is a further salutary reminder of the accelerating pace of change and, consequently, the contracting lead-time for adaptation, that the introduction of increasingly sophisticated systems has closely paralleled the continuous shift to larger stores. If it took a millenium to develop the abacus, and a century the manual till, then the electronic cash register came of age in less than a decade – and is already threatened with obsolescence by the introduction first of bar coding, and now with the Electronic Point of Sale (EPOS) systems, which additionally make possible automatic stocktaking, essential in a huge store.

Individually either of the developments – much larger stores or advanced electronic systems – would have posed problems. Together they created the very real risk of depersonalising shopping, of intimidating and thus alienating the customer. Certainly in-store design can do much to overcome the problem. But in the end the character of The Shop, whatever its form, continues to depend on the quality of its staff, which explains the growing stress placed on the recruitment and the training of all levels of staff within the company.

Seen from the distance of a decade, Tesco's revival may appear as a seamless pattern, each element reinforcing the other – selling in the new identity, reorienting the development programme to complement this image, introducing increasingly refined systems to service the new generation of large stores, and, above all, training a new generation of staff to manage them. As we've seen, things were not quite so controlled. Theoretically of course a comprehensive strategy for the management of change *should* have been formulated before the launch of Checkout. But there is a world of difference between theory and practice, and even the most optimistic could not have anticipated the extraordinary success of the operation.

True, the Board calculated on an increase in turnover – otherwise the Checkout decision would never have been taken. True, dispositions were made for managing this expansion, for employing extra staff, for distributing the increased volume of goods – otherwise the operation would not have been the success it was. True, there was a widespread if inchoate recognition of the need to develop a new and coherent trading philosophy – otherwise one would never have emerged. Initially the process may have been piecemeal. Gradually, however, it gained in definition, and it was here that the attitude of upper management was crucial.

The inherent risk of success is that it can all too easily induce complacency, a corrosive condition in any business, and in the retail sector a fatal one. There can be no doubts at all about the impact of Checkout, as indicated by the near-frenzied response of the com-, petition. As the *Financial Times* reported, there was 'war on the High Street', and for Tesco two priorities emerged – to consolidate on immediate gains while developing a credible formula for future expansion. Both ultimately turned on the capacity of senior management to rethink its entire approach to the company.

Where previously senior management had tended to live on a day-to-day basis, depending on 'feel' for the market, there was now to be a significant shift towards 'thinking long'. Consideration not only had to be given to trading conditions within retailing itself, but also to a range of external factors (economic, social, technological, political) that determine retail performance – factors over which we can exert little, if any control, yet which have a powerful shaping effect on the whole character of our business.

There was (and in some cases continues to be) a deep-rooted belief among certain retailers that they shaped, rather than were shaped by, the environment in which they traded. The notion, by no means confined to retailers, is absurd. No company is bigger than the market in which it trades, and unless it makes an effort to gain some idea of what the future may hold, it radically diminishes its future trading prospects. So much may be self-evident, but the practice of regarding the present as a touchstone for the future remains commonplace – yet another, and potentially fatal, legacy of success.

What was true in the past is doubly true today, when market conditions are changing with increasing rapidity. Once, possibly, there was time to adjust to change, to take a relaxed view of emergent developments, confident that time was at a discount. No longer. Retailing development – from the self-service store of the 1940s to the supermarket of the 1950s and 1960s, to today's so-called 'large store' – indicates graphically both the accelerating pace of change and the foreshortened time for adjustment. In short, time is now at a premium, and will continue to be so into the foreseeable future.

Thus, the capacity to 'think long' becomes central to the formulation of strategy. Encouragingly even the Chancellor, Nigel Lawson, has now become a convert to the discipline, if his criticism of what he calls 'short termism' is to be believed. Tesco anticipated his conversion by more than a decade, for within months of the launch of Checkout, our Chairman at the time, Sir Leslie Porter, was reflecting to the Market Research Society: 'Obviously no one should diminish the importance of market research though, in doing so, we should never neglect the longer time horizon . . . the future is out there, waiting for us. It is essential to try and understand what it holds, rather than waiting to be overtaken by events.'

Sir Leslie's comment provided an insight into the emergence of a new philosophy within the company which was to have profound implications for the future. At one level of course the notion is a contradiction in terms. At another it is an explicit recognition of the impossibility of attempting to manage by objectives when the objectives are conditioned by external factors over which management exerts only marginal control.

Obviously there are no absolutes in the game of strategic planning. As Tesco has learned, however, this does nothing to minimise its importance. Indeed, without the capacity to monitor and then interpret the underlying shifts taking place in the socio-economy, all the internal changes (the creation of a new identity, the development of new stores, the retraining of staff, the application of advanced systems) are placed in jeopardy.

Not that the external and internal elements are incompatible. On the contrary, they complement one another to provide a coherent strategy for trading in tomorrow's world: a strategy based on identifying on the one hand where the company should be going, and on the other how it is to get there. The alternative, of being taken unawares by what Galbraith once termed 'The Uncertain Future', is at best a high-risk formula, and at worst a self-destruct mechanism of corporate magnitude.

In Tesco's case the lesson of attempting to manage the future and, consequently, of managing change took time to learn. To pretend otherwise would be nonsense. Traditional attitudes and practices die hard, and it has taken time to reorient the company since the exciting days of 1977. More importantly, the reorientation process still continues, as is inevitable if the company is to show it has gleaned anything from the past.

Nothing succeeds like success, they say, but history has an equally full portfolio of evidence to the contrary: nothing has been known to fail like success either. Success is a risky business. Within itself it carries the seeds of failure – complacency, ignorance and a lightheaded arrogance. Behind some of the world's most spectacular failures lies a blissful optimism born of earlier success.

My own company, Tesco, provides the perfect example: steady, seemingly inexorable progress for 50 years, with success after stunning success, and then, in the mid-1970s, the shocking realisation that nobody – neither the consumer nor the money market – wanted to know any more. Dr Johnson once described what follows success as 'that empty sound'. It is the point at which, as we at Tesco have now learned the hard way, success must be redefined. New criteria must be established by which to measure it. For those in business, and British industry in particular, I'd say it's sufficiently dangerous to warrant a warning: 'Handle with Care: Success can Seriously Damage Your Health (and the national economy)'.

14 Fiat

by Cesare Romiti,
Managing Director, FIAT SPA

The turnaround at Fiat has often been referred to as a miracle. At the same time the recovery of the Italian economy has usually been described by way of jargon widely linked to religious works. However, the U-turn which happened at Fiat at the beginning of the decade was not due to divine intervention. It was the result of a consistent, all-out effort to bring about the industrial, economic and financial recovery of the Fiat Group, Italy's largest private concern.

Though we supposedly live in an age of communications, clichés and stereotypes still abound. It is time to look below the surface of the Italian political, industrial and commercial scene and try to understand the true situation according to accurate scientific parameters, abandoning the old traditional myths.

For example, it has been said and written repeatedly that one of the main reasons for the weakness of Fiat in the 1970s was the strategy of diversification out of the core automotive business. This idea originates from a misinterpretation of the reorganisation of Fiat Group structure which was carried out between 1974 and 1979. The aim behind the new structure was to establish a more manageable industrial organisation, in which the decision-making process could become less complex and more efficient.

The Fiat Group broke down its monolithic structure into twelve main operating sectors, all under the umbrella of one parent company, Fiat SpA. This created a more flexible concern. It brought about the rationalisation of those sectors that were not well integrated into the system, the strengthening of weaker sectors, and a structure that made international alliances more flexible.

The formation of Iveco in 1975 did not mean that Fiat had decided to enter the truck business at that time. In fact Fiat's first commercial vehicle dates back to 1903. Iveco, a truly pan-European company, in which Unic of France and Magirus Deutz of West Germany truck operations were combined with the Fiat, OM and Lancia commercial vehicle activities, is a typical example of the strategy adopted by Fiat to broaden its European base. The last piece of the jigsaw was added in 1986 with a joint venture with the British truck sector of Ford.

This policy was applied broadly throughout the Fiat Group, especially to areas of business in which Fiat was established before the Second World War: from agriculture to construction machinery, aviation to metallurgy and so on (see Table 14.1).

Far from diversifying away from its core business, Fiat in the 1970s actually withdrew from some areas of activity. The production of steel was abandoned, and a joint venture for large marine engines as well as a similar venture for the manufacture of aircraft bodies were terminated. Nevertheless Fiat continued operating successfully in project design, development and production of jet engines. Fiat Aviation participates in several major international aerospace ventures with leading companies, including Pratt & Whitney, Rolls-Royce, General Electric and MTU.

These misconceptions which surround the Fiat Group still survive despite clear evidence to the contrary.

In the second half of the 1970s Italy was plagued with a disturbing disease. The international economic scenario had undergone a number of extreme changes, which were particularly unfavourable to industry. Inflation in Italy was far above the already high level reached in other European countries. Uncontrolled growth of public expenditure had led to heavy budget deficits, and financing the deficit was a major source of inflation and misallocation of resources.

Private enterprises had to compete with the public sector for the scarce resources available: thus the cost of capital for private enterprises was prohibitive. Moreover the two oil shocks had caused a deterioration of the balance of payments and disrupted the automotive market.

Fiat had to contend not only with market difficulties but also with a worsening social climate. Social tensions, unreasonable demands by unions, dissatisfaction with work, as well as political instability gave rise to wildcat strikes and troubles at many of our plants. Product quality deteriorated. Absenteeism exceeded 20 per cent. Violence and intimidation by small extremist fringes was rampant.

Social unrest, together with political instability, had sown the seeds of terrorism; and Fiat, because of its unique role within the industrial and

TABLE 14.1

Year	Fiat's progress
1899	First Fiat automobile, the 4HP
1901	First collective transport vehicle, the omnibus
1903	First commercial vehicle
1905	First marine engine
1906	First tram powered by a gasoline engine
1907	First diesel engine built
1908	First aero engine
1908	First Lancia car
1912	Start of public transport business
1912	Fiat Lubrificanti set up
1915	The first military aeroplane is built
1917	Fiat starts railway production systems
1917	Fiat joins the metallurgy sector
1918	First wheeled agricultural tractor
1919	Fiat starts producing motor-vehicle components
1922	The first diesel engine electric railway is built
1929	Impresit set up: Fiat enters the civil engineering world
1930	First Fiat engine to be fitted into a helicopter
1930	First direct injection diesel truck engine
1930	World's first internal combustion locomotive
1932	Fiat agricultural crawler tractor
1934	Fiat becomes active in the tourist sector
1950	Start of construction machinery production
1951	Italy's first jet plane produced
1956	Fiat joins the nuclear sector
1957	Gas turbine production is launched
1967	Bioengineering production begins
1968	Space research
1974	The first welding robot at Mirafiori Bodyworks
1976	Fiat buys Telettra and moves into telecommunications
1977	The first artificial heart valve is implanted
1978	Comau produces the first ever robotised car body system
1979	The first programmable pacemaker
1980	The first robot with telecamera goes into production
1981	Comau produces the first robotised auto engineering system
1985	Termoli 3, the world's most highly automated auto engineering factory goes into operation
1986	Two-millionth Uno produced

business scene, became a special target for terrorism. Fiat managers' lives were at risk, and in fact four executives were shot dead and twenty-seven wounded. A complex web of political, social and economic factors had pushed Fiat into a corner.

It was an almost impossible situation. Fiat was described as on the ropes and ready for receivership or as being about to fall prey to government intervention.

But the wounded company fought back.

A few data may be useful to illustrate the magnitude of the 'turn-around' and thus the magnitude of the problems. (In detail see Tables 14.2 and 14.3, financial highlights and financial ratios.)

In the period 1981–6 the Fiat Group:

- increased turnover by 44 per cent

- reduced the workforce by 31 per cent

- invested 9.3 billion dollars in capital expenditure

- spent 3.9 billion dollars on R&D programmes

- reduced its net indebtedness by 897 per cent to 530 million dollars

- improved its net income twenty-three times

- increased productivity by manufacturing workers from 14.8 cars in 1979 to 29 per worker in 1986

These results were not achieved by a miracle. The strategies adopted bear witness to an all-out effort.

Industrial risk had to be reduced. Production capability was concentrated and redeployed. Extensive innovation in production systems was introduced, while automation and flexibility in all our plants was increased.

Costs had to come down. With a stagnant market and fierce competition, survival depended on producing competitive products at the lowest possible costs. Productivity had to increase, and quality had to improve.

A thorough in-depth review was carried out within the twelve main areas of business in which Fiat operates, to lower the break-even point. Between 1980 and 1986 the break-even point of Fiat's automobile operation dropped by almost 30 per cent and the break-even point of Fiat's truck division, Iveco, was trimmed by over 40 per cent. All sectors were restructured and in 1986–7 the break-even level was about one-third lower than it was 6 years before.

An aggressive investment programme was implemented, to renovate and improve production systems and to modernise the range of products both in the automotive sector and in our other businesses.

TABLE 14.2 *Financial highlights (US $m)*

	1986	1985	1984	1983	1982	1981
Net sales and revenues	22,041	20,361	17,891	16,517	15,491	15,260
Depreciation and amortisation	1,190	1,150	1,096	912	757	713
Operating income	1,845	1,703	1,401	978	909	1,152
Financial (costs) income	58.5	524	644	746	759	1,179
Income before taxes	2,234	1,263	653	282	196	140
Net income	1,624	996	471	190	102	67
Cash flow	2,964	2,228	1,609	1,105	858	725
Capital expenditure	2,163	1,076	1,116	1,091	988	614
R&D expenditure	717	616	502	417	375	308
Net indebtedness	530	1,776	3,037	4,057	4,634	5,285
Stockholders' equity	7,527	5,488	4,747	3,836	3,683	2,696
No. of employees	230,293	226,222	230,805	243,808	263,760	301,658

TABLE 14.3 *Significant financial ratios (%)*

	1986	1985	1984	1983	1982	1981
Operating income/net sales and revenues	8.4	8.4	7.8	5.9	5.9	7.6
Operating income/capital invested (net)	17.0	17.6	14.2	10.0	9.1	12.2
Income before taxes/net sales and revenues	10.1	6.2	3.7	1.7	1.3	0.9
Income before minority interests/net sales and revenues	8.0	5.3	2.9	1.2	0.7	0.1
Net income/stockholders' equity	21.6	18.2	9.9	5.0	2.8	2.5
Financial (costs) income/net sales and revenues	0.3	(2.6)	(3.6)	(4.5)	(4.9)	(7.7)
Depreciation and amortisation/net sales and revenues	5.4	5.7	6.1	5.5	4.9	4.7
Cash flow/net sales and revenues	13.4	10.9	8.9	6.7	5.6	4.8
Gross additions to plant, property and equipment plus R&D/net sales and revenues	13.1	8.3	9.1	9.1	8.8	6.0
Net indebtedness/stockholders' minority equity	0.06/1	0.29/1	0.59/1	0.97/1	1.2/1	1.9/1

Several car models of totally new conception were designed and introduced in rapid succession. Fiat's car product range is currently the most advanced and youngest in Europe.

First of all, however, Fiat took several decisive steps. Thus senior management became rather unpopular, not only with the unions but also with political parties and opinion leaders.

In 1979 sixty-one known troublemakers were fired. This was unheard of in Italy and reactions varied between shock and outrage. A confrontation with the trade unions ensued and pressure was exerted to force the company to rehire them. Later a massive lay-off of workers followed. This was the beginning of a 35-day strike, with frequent episodes of violence and intolerance. More pressure to induce Fiat to take a 'soft line' and cancel the lay-offs was exercised.

But Fiat refused to compromise. There was no choice, for the survival of the corporation was at stake. In addition, the re-establishment of rationality in the management of the economy was at risk. If Fiat could not restore a measure of sanity to the national economy, then nobody else could. But if Fiat succeeded, the others would follow.

An extreme risk was taken, but there again, there was no alternative although several observers and many trade unionists did not understand what was at stake. Though the majority of the workers were confused, intimidated and frightened, they were still committed to certain moral values and to the company. This perception was very clear in the minds of the Fiat managers.

Furthermore, Fiat felt that the extreme and unreasonable attitudes of fringe groups and trade unions did not reflect either the interests or the needs of most workers. This point proved to be correct. After a 5-week strike, more than 40,000 Fiat employees, both white- and blue-collar workers, marched through the streets of Turin demanding the right to return to work.

That day, 14 October 1980, represented a watershed not only for Fiat, but for Italy. From that moment on industrial relations and the social climate in Italy changed radically for the better, and the positive effect of this transformation has been maintained in time. This was the fundamental event that gave rise both to Fiat's turnaround and indeed to that of Italy. It was the essential condition that allowed all other measures to be applied and be successful.

The lay-offs of 1980 were not linked to the weakness of the market, or to a movement along the cost curve, but to a shift in the cost curve towards a different production function. New production systems had to be introduced. This called for a massive investment programme, and large financial resources had to be secured.

A substantial increase in share capital was announced almost at the same time as the lay-offs. Capital stock was more than doubled.

The Fiat move was read as a turning point and not as a defensive move. In one of the few multinationals in which the founding family retains a major shareholding the announcement of an increase in share capital was perceived as an assurance of continuity, as a proof of deep confidence in the future of the company and as a commitment by the Agnelli family and other shareholders to its survival and expansion.

In turn the recapitalisation of Fiat was made necessary by a radical rethinking of the prospects for the automotive industry and was directed towards an extensive retooling of the production lines. Current techniques made this possible, through modernisation and automation. Fiat had already experimented in the mid-1970s with factory automation, and was, as a result, a leader in the field through its subsidiary Comau.

In-house know-how made it possible to set an ambitious target: Fiat was to become a model carmaker, leading the way in flexible manufacturing systems as applied to car production. The number of robots employed in Fiat's factories rose from 230 to 1,050 and has reached 1,600 in 1988. These robots, mainly manufactured by Comau, represent about 50 per cent of the total number of robots installed in Italy.

Automation was necessary to improve productivity, standardisation and product quality, and to eliminate hazardous and unpleasant jobs, thus improving working conditions in the plants. Extensive introduction of automated systems also modified the structure of employment. Unskilled jobs were replaced by skilled jobs, which required extensive retraining of workers.

Flexibility is one of the key factors in automation. It is known that robotisation enhances the advantages of the assembly line, yielding more mileage out of the mass production process. Nevertheless this is only one aspect of factory automation. The use of programmable robots now allows repetitive operations to be switched back and forth from one model to another, so that an assembly line no longer needs to be specific to one model but can manufacture different car models without any retooling or loss of time.

The process of automation at Fiat has proceeded steadily in the last 6 years and will continue at a fast pace. Automation is not limited to replacing men with robots. It starts at the drawing board. Parts and components are designed to be handled by robots and to be assembled with maximum speed and efficiency.

From the manufacturing viewpoint the most recent accomplishment by Fiat is the new family of engines called 'Fire' (Fully Integrated Robotised Engine). This new engine family was conceived and designed in tandem with the manufacturing plant producing it at Termoli, in the south of Italy.

These systematic integrated principles are being applied in other areas of operations. At the beginning of 1987 Fiat and IBM announced a joint venture, the first in the world to offer a comprehensive communications network for managing and controlling stocks. The venture will provide a computerised exchange of information between suppliers, manufacturers, transport distributors and points of sale of the finished product. The aim is to reduce working capital tied up in manufacturing and distribution through more efficient management of resources.

The shift towards more capital and less labour was accomplished by a review of Fiat's presence worldwide. Given the new priorities, it was realised that Fiat was geographically overextended, both in terms of production and in terms of markets. As a result, Fiat has concentrated on Europe, which is considered the domestic market. Among others, the decision was reached to pull out of the car business in the United States, except for the lucrative Ferrari operation. It was a difficult and painful decision. But by the early 1980s Fiat's presence there was absorbing too many managerial and financial resources, owing to production costs and network problems – a situation common to European mass producers operating in the States.

The fact that Fiat Auto has subsequently become market leader and the most profitable carmaker in Europe proves that the right decision was taken in 1982. Incidentally, such a step has been imitated by other European companies.

More generally, Fiat's guiding principle at the beginning of the 1980s was to ignore questions of prestige and image and to concentrate ruthlessly on costs and benefits. If Fiat's presence in a given market was not profitable, we would pull out, ignoring history and tradition.

In South America several operations were sold off or closed down, except the one in Brazil. Thus the Brazilian operation became the major car-manufacturing affiliate of Fiat abroad.

The geographical reorganisation of Fiat's presence stemmed from an evaluation of the strengths and weaknesses of our market share. Fiat, unlike other companies, had an exceedingly strong national position.

No other car, truck, or agricultural equipment maker had such a dominant position in its own country. It was thus essential, for a company bent on restructuring, to start from home base, to strengthen its core business. Only after having once again secured its hold on the domestic market could Fiat again widen its horizons.

The first stage of the new strategy meant that we had to lower our sights. This called for a cautious approach to Europe and for a hard look at the more distant branches of the widespread Group.

Four other areas in Fiat's overhaul must be mentioned. They are inventories, dealers, suppliers and finance.

While work-in-process depends on actual production, input and output inventories can be minimised. A reorganisation of the various production stages and stricter requirements for suppliers' delivery schedules enabled Fiat to create its own version of the Japanese just-in-time procedures for inventory control.

Inventories of finished products were lowered year after year. In addition, the financing of dealers' stocks was to be borne by the dealer himself. The shift of the financing burden was part of a wider effort to encourage the dealers' entrepreneurial traits and aggressiveness. The dominant position of Fiat in Italy had transformed many dealers into 'car brokers', but the new contractual arrangements changed the situation: dealers had to become more 'sales minded'.

The system of suppliers is a crucial determinant of a manufacturing company's performance. The number of suppliers was reduced. The use of common components on different products was increased. Moreover Fiat's considerable bargaining power was fully used in forcing suppliers to supply at low prices and therefore to introduce measures to cut their own costs. Fiat's cost-cutting thus was felt through the whole industry. Leaner and more efficient suppliers emerged. A domino effect in industrial restructuring resulted.

Cuts in inventories and stricter control of suppliers allowed reductions in working capital. Capital investment per unit of output decreased considerably – a textbook reaction to the high cost of capital which prevailed at the time and which of course still prevails. This reduction in working capital was all the more urgent as Italian manufacturers were relatively at a disadvantage *vis-à-vis* their competitors.

Centralisation of finances in the holding company of the Fiat Group (of which Fiat Auto is the largest subsidiary) was an essential move to achieve optimum management of cash flow. Strict control on the use of scarce financial resources was introduced. Successful efforts were made to minimise the cost of borrowed funds and to maximise return on liquidity. An extensive network of financial affiliates was created to provide dealer and retail financing.

Consistent efforts were made during this period to strengthen the Group equity base. Following the capital increase of 1980, Fiat carried out new capital increases in 1984 and 1986 for a total of about $1.4 billion.

At the same time a number of the most profitable companies in the Group, including Sorin Biomedica (bioengineering), Comau (production systems) and Fidis (an investment finance company) were quoted on the Stock Exchange. The objective was to expand the equity base of the Group, though maintaining majority control of the corporations. All these points summarise the basic strategy adopted by Fiat in what was the first phase of the turnaround.

The second phase, which began in 1986, is going to be a phase of expansion. In meeting the challenges of this next period Fiat will base its strategies on the strengths reacquired during recent years:

- ample and stable earnings and cash flow
- solid financial structure
- innovative and advanced technology

Starting from these strong points, our strategies will be aimed at:

- maintaining and improving our earnings and financial performance
- exploiting opportunities for expansion
- accelerating the process of internationalisation
- promoting innovation and maintaining high technological standards

In 1986 Fiat reaffirmed that the Group is basically an automotive group, and it will remain so in the future. The acquisition of Alfa Romeo and the joint venture in Britain between the truck division of Ford and the Fiat commercial vehicle division, Iveco, confirms this. However, it is widely accepted that in the years to come the automotive industry will not be among the fastest growing businesses, and that the new emergent high-tech industries will represent an increasing share of advanced economies. Therefore in the 1990s Fiat will move more and more into high-tech sectors, and become more international in its market horizons and more multinational in its production and organisational structures.

Fiat's future trends can be defined as 'selective development'. On the one hand this means the capacity to consolidate the sectors where the Group is structurally strong. On the other, it implies developing the sectors where Fiat subsidiaries already have the basic conditions for success but have not yet reached adequate dimensions. It means Fiat must keep in the vanguard in the race towards innovation and technology.

Specifically Fiat will:

- work on international co-operation in automotive components (e.g. with Matra and Lucas) and production systems (with GM in the USA)

- increase synergies

- develop space and defence technologies and products, telecommunications, bioengineering and aviation

- enlarge the business of finance and credit companies and other value-added services

- strengthen its presence in Europe, which is considered Fiat's domestic market, and selectively expand our presence in other areas.

Fiat has already set the stage for this programme in the following fashion:

- In partnership with United Technologies, a share in Westland, the British helicopter manufacturer, was acquired.

- The acquisition of the operating control of SNIA-BPD has expanded Fiat's space and defence activities and provided an important technological base in fibres and composite materials.

- A number of joint ventures have been formed or are being contemplated by Telettra, the telecommunications unit.

- A Fiat majority-owned venture with Matra has acquired control of

Jaeger and Solex, thus achieving significant economies of scale and reinforcing Fiat's market position in the European automotive components business. This process was further enhanced by the recent agreement with Lucas in England and Carello in Italy.

- In the field of construction equipment a joint venture has been formed with Hitachi for the development and manufacture of hydraulic excavators.

- In the truck business the Iveco–Ford Truck Ltd joint venture and the more recent acquisition of Astra have reinforced and enlarged the European dimension.

- Fiatagri and Iveco signed two important agreements with China which will greatly expand Fiat's presence in the major markets of Asia. The projects, which comprise transfer of technology, technical assistance, and training, will result in the restructuring of a number of plants in which Fiat trucks and agricultural tractors will be manufactured under licence.

- Last but not least, the acquisition of Alfa Romeo and its merger with Lancia will permit Fiat to become leader in the luxury car market, which currently represents 1.8 million units in Europe, or about 16 per cent of total sales, and is the fastest growing segment of the market. The newly born Alfa–Lancia Corporation already has a market share well above 20 per cent in this market. When the challenging task of its restructuring and reorganisation is completed, it is expected that its position will be further improved.

These achievements and the targets set before the company cannot be appreciated without considering the role of management. In the last few years Fiat has concentrated great effort on innovation and on management development. It has created organisational and management systems, expanded training centres, and developed a common culture and a modern and loyal multinational professionalism.

Fiat is determined to continue improving its already streamlined organisation and to pay great attention to the development of human resources. In this revolution of new technologies, products, systems, financial methods and business opportunities, the development of human resources is the most delicate aspect of the Group's strategy.

Fiat is well aware of the difficulties that lie ahead, but experience in the past few years has proved, first and foremost to the management, that success can be achieved even in extremely difficult circumstances. Fiat is confident that as long as the company's most important resource – people – maintain their commitment to the company, with ability, creativity, flexibility and courage, Fiat can face the future and its new challenges with prudent but with well founded optimism.

15 Woolworth Holdings

by Geoffrey Mulcahy,
Chief Executive, WOOLWORTH HOLDINGS PLC

At 9.45am on 15 November 1982 four men, directors of Paternoster Stores, met in London's Marylebone Station coffee bar. They had an appointment up the road 15 minutes later. It was a momentous occasion. The meeting was to be the first with the old board of F. W. Woolworth, the retailing colossus that had just been bought out by our new company.

Paternoster Stores had been formed in September that year. It was a novel and bold initiative that had been mooted by a number of leading figures in the City and in the property business, and brought to fruition by Victor Blank, then head of Corporate Finance of Charterhouse (address: Paternoster Square). They had spotted the possibility of turning round the high-street giant which had been underperforming for years after decades of glorious success. F. W. Woolworth had lost its way in the retailing scene of the 1970s, and become a misery stock for its ever hopeful shareholders. Yet it had one great strength: its huge property folio. It could never sink with the buoyancy provided by such assets, whose value was twice the company's capitalisation. But it was doing the next best thing to sinking – it was floundering badly.

F. W. Woolworth was big by any standard. In terms of its sales space it was twice the size of Sainsbury's today. It had become so on a mass-merchandising formula, forged in the USA, which had flourished particularly well in Britain. For 50 years it had been brilliantly successful, playing a unique role in the life and affections of the nation; but from the late 1950s things gradually began to go wrong. The first visible sign of trouble came in 1968, when F. W. Woolworth lost its place as Britain's leading retailer and Marks & Spencer overhauled it in both sales and profits.

During the 1970s its burgeoning problems really began to get worse.

The problems were of its own making. A formula that had served so well for so long had become enshrined. When confronted by change, the ability to respond was subverted by an internally bred management and burdensome bureaucracy, which only understood one way of doing things; and change was the order of the day in the 1970s. Store concepts were changing rapidly, and customer expectations with them.

F. W. Woolworth did recognise the need for change. Some new initiatives were taken, but their implementation failed under a management inadequate for the task. The Woolco stores had been a golden opportunity for the company to take the lead in the supermarket scene. Modelled on US experience, ten Woolco stores were opened in Britain on edge-of-town sites. But the company failed to make the concept distinct. The same buyers were employed as for the F. W. Woolworth stores, so the same kind of merchandise turned up at the Woolco stores. Customers were confused by what Woolco was meant to be. There was a lesson here for us, one which we learnt and applied later in our turnaround strategy.

Towards the end of the old regime the board of F. W. Woolworth did make a decision that had the promise of success, and one that was to have great significance later on in a way that could not have been imagined then: the board, encouraged by its US parent, decided in 1981 to buy the fledgling B&Q operation for £17m. Such was the scepticism of the shareholders and markets by that time that the move was criticised – the cost was too high, B&Q was irrelevant to the company's problems anyway, etc. etc.

It was against this background of disenchantment that the Paternoster Stores offer was judged. The British F. W. Woolworth was 52 per cent owned by its US counterpart; the remainder was owned by institutions and private shareholders. Paternoster Stores paid £310m for the company, whose equity weakness was revealed by the split: £100m capital and £210m debt. It was the first highly leveraged buyout in Britain.

Sensing the mood of the existing directors, one financial adviser recommended the board to advise shareholders to take the cash offer – but subsequently, after the bid succeeded, its investment management arm actually bought 14 per cent of the equity. In fact over 95 per cent of institutional and private shareholders sold, only too glad to be rid of stock that had failed them for so long.

The Paternoster deal was backed by thirty institutions. But perhaps because of its novelty or because the turnaround task was thought to be impossible, or because the new board was not well endowed with specialist retailers, not many people gave it much of a chance.

But we had other ideas: no magic formulae or dramatic strategies, but the ability and will to apply classic turnaround principles and the recognition that it would take, above all, hard work and stamina. What we took over was frankly a chaotic management. We found a filing cabinet full of recovery strategies recommending dramatic courses of action. It was a case of management suffering from a severe bout of 'analysis paralysis'.

The US parent, with its 52 per cent shareholding, had had the legal control to do something about the problems, but, beset by its own troubles, it did not have the credibility with British management to dictate solutions. With no apparent objectives, staff morale was at rock bottom. There were 50,000 staff in the chain, which consisted of nearly 1,000 stores ranging from 2,000 square feet to 70,000 square feet in locations whose quality varied tremendously. Some were in prime high-street sites, others in dying suburban strips and edge-of-town sites. The warehouses and stockrooms were crammed with £500m worth of stock. The stores sold over 50,000 lines through sixty-two departments, dealt with 8,000 suppliers and processed over six million invoices averaging under £10 in value. The average customer spent just £1.

There was no real management information: there was that £500m stock figure and a gross figure of sales to date, but there was no information on what the stock comprised, what was selling, where the company was making money, or where the company was losing money. We did know, however, that the average £1-spending customer was multiplied by well over 10 million – an astounding loyalty in the circumstances.

The first task was obvious and urgent. Without delay, a new top management team was assembled. Paternoster Stores became Woolworth Holdings, and thus a totally new board took over from day one. The next priority was to institute a firm financial hold on the business and start creating order out of the chaos. In the following 2–3 months a number of critical decisions were made. At the top level we established the group structure. Woolworth Holdings became the new parent, with F. W. Woolworth, B&Q and Woolworth Properties as operating subsidiaries.

After a thorough review of B&Q we decided to redeploy capital to support its rapid growth and seize the out-of-town DIY market, whose potential its management had already identified. Systems were already in place to keep B&Q completely separate from F. W. Woolworth. This was a crucial strategy. B&Q's profit potential was enormous and immediate; its success could buy us the time we needed to deal with the more problematical F. W. Woolworth chain. Thus the acquisition of B&Q by the old regime turned out to be fortunate for us.

The property company, Woolworth Properties, was set up to manage the huge property asset. By charging market rents to F. W. Woolworth we were able to ascertain where our profits were coming from – retailing or property.

As for F. W. Woolworth itself, comprehensive reorganisation was required; and just as important, a total change in the attitude of staff. We established firm financial controls. We set about reducing stocks and cutting costs. We reorganised the management structure, eliminating the layer upon layer of regional and area management and shortening lines of communication.

We opened up lines of communication with employees and trade unions. They knew only too well that the company had problems and were not surprised that we recognised them. They did, however, feel the distinct change in management style when we started communicating with them about our problems. We made it clear to them that we were not in the business of asset-stripping, but were determined on a turn-around of the business which would require their understanding and positive response. That is what they gave us.

During 1983, as B&Q rapidly expanded under its energetic and cap-able management, we went about the major task of developing a formula for trading in the F. W. Woolworth stores that would increase their profitability substantially. We decided on a number of strategies that would be implemented together and at once. Thus we strengthened and improved further financial controls by introducing budgeting and re-porting procedures in order to accelerate both cost reductions and give us detailed sales, margin and stock information. None of these systems existed!

At the same time we recruited a new management team to give us professionals in all key positions. F. W. Woolworth's main management problem was that virtually everybody there had never worked anywhere else. They knew only one creed, the gospel according to Woolworth, and that had been discredited. There was little or no depth of professional management in systems, distribution, finance or even, believe it or not, marketing.

Another early decision was to reduce stocks and introduce improved, centralised distribution and systems. This included long overdue con-trols on suppliers, some of whom delivered in days but others in months. We also continued to improve our communications efforts at all levels, and set about changing the historic pay and incentives schemes to rid the business of practices open to abuse. In their place we introduced schemes designed to motivate, with incentive pay systems and stock options. When we introduced our share option scheme in 1983, we had one of the highest take-ups in the history of such schemes.

Throughout this period – the first 2 years – all these things were being directed by a very small team of three or four people, of whom I was one. We had to keep our shareholders informed of our progress, and after an all too brief honeymoon, we had to live under constant pressure for tangible results, as well as the continuing scepticism that had characterised the reaction to the original buyout. They were long days and nights.

At the end of our 1983–4 accounting period we reported a fivefold increase in group profits, with F. W. Woolworth's contribution up from £900,000 to £7.6m, and B&Q's up from £9.1m to £19.3m. We were not discouraged.

Neither were we complacent. There was a great deal to do before we could claim any kind of turnaround. So we embarked on a new phase of development in our second full year. The main ingredients of this were the continued development of B&Q; the addition of a new company, Comet, to the group; the rationalisation of Woolworth Properties' store portfolio; and, most important of all, the development of a new, marketing-led strategy for F. W. Woolworth.

The new addition to the Woolworth Holdings group, Comet, had proved itself profitable in merchandising home electronics and electrical goods, and had built up a reputation for value amongst its customers. We saw its potential as an out-of-town operation in a market that was set to expand, and as a complement to our other retail operations and expertise. With the potential but not the capital to change and grow, Comet was in the market. We won it – not to rapturous applause but more an attitude of 'let's wait and see' from the pundits.

As for F. W. Woolworth, the chain had been trying to be all things to all people for too long – a Jack-of-all-trades and definitely master of none. There was no easily identifiable part of the business whose closure or sale would benefit the other parts automatically. What we had to do was to take fundamental decisions affecting every aspect of the business. During 1984 we began the process of focusing down through the chain. We went even further the following year.

At the same time we set up a special project called 'Weekend and General' to test an even more radical concept, comprising a strengthened merchandise range, retrained staff and a new store design, culminating in what was a new offer to the customer. It meant eliminating a large part of the existing range and radically improving the new areas in which we chose to concentrate. The project was directed by specialists outside the day-to-day operation and was under my personal control. It was the start of the new 'Woolworths'.

We dropped the cumbersome 'F. W. Woolworth' as a signal that changes in the stores were fundamental. The special project had showed we were ready for a more general implementation. Already the profitability of the stores – up £22m by the spring of 1986 – had shown the fruits of focusing down through the chain.

Now a full blown 'Operation Focus' was instituted. It meant concentrating in areas where Woolworths had established strengths, and developing real authority in them through broader ranges, better quality and brighter stores. The six areas of focus in which Woolworths is a major player in the market and has full credibility are Kids (we are one of Britain's biggest toy shops), Gifts and Sweets (we are a European leader of confectionery outlets), Entertainment (we are a market leader in recorded entertainment), Home and Garden (we are a clear leader in the high street), Kitchens (a traditional Woolworths strength) and Looks (an opportunity to capitalise on our young female shoppers).

Thus we now have six market-led departments compared with the sixty-two we inherited, 20,000 lines compared with 50,000, and 1,000 key suppliers compared with 8,000. We spent £40m in 1986 introducing the new Woolworths in over 140 of our remaining 818 high-street stores.

Turnarounds classically include cutting back, and this we have done in Woolworths. We have totally withdrawn from grocery, adult clothes, electrical appliances and a number of other areas – in all a sacrifice of some £250m or 25 per cent of our high-street turnover. But the cuts have made way for our Focus departments to expand.

The Woolworths' turnaround has been huge by any standards. It was perhaps Dixon's £1.8 billion bid in 1986 that tested its reality. Our successful defence was, and remains, the largest to date in Britain. It highlighted the fact that the original 1982 dream had become reality, and that Woolworth is no longer a turnaround company.

Since then the group has continued its rapid progress. B&Q has continued to expand and is developing other concepts alongside its DIY stores. The acquisition of the Charlie Browns Autocentres has created an opportunity in the car servicing and accessories market. Comet has been repositioned as an out-of-town store chain with new merchandise

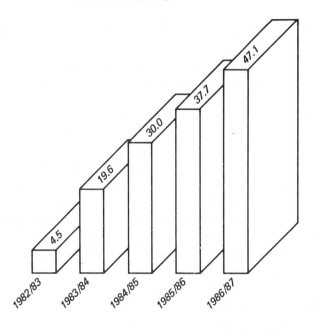

FIGURE 15.1 *Earnings per share, before exceptional items (pence), 1982–7.*

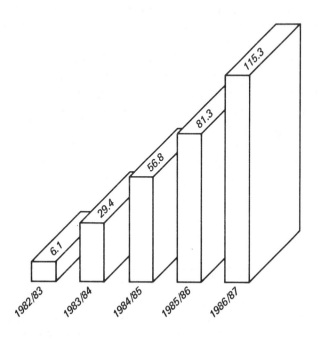

FIGURE 15.2 *Pre-tax profit, before exceptional items (£m), 1982–7.*

ranges and livelier stores. Woolworths has accelerated its Focus programme and opened its special Kidstores for 2–13 year olds. Woolworth
Properties is working with Rosehaugh, a leading developer, to maximise
the potential of the property assets. Another company, Superdrug, has
also joined the group, giving it a market niche in the drugstore supermarket format pioneered by the company.

The group structure is now firmly established, with the Woolworth
Holdings management and board determining the strategy and agreeing
the medium-term plans and annual budgets, monitoring performance
and allocating capital. It will continue to pursue specialist strategies for
the operating companies, and look for new areas and opportunities for
specialism within our business and elsewhere in the marketplace.

What we have achieved has been due to three prime ingredients: the
ability to be clinically objective in analysing and taking decisions, the
willingness to take radical decisions and to implement them vigorously,
and the understanding of the importance of communications – with
staff, with customers, with shareholders.

The yardstick of our achievement is the growth of our earnings per
share (Figure 15.1). At mid-1987 we were in the top three quoted
companies in the growth league of earnings per share. Since 1982 our
earnings have increased 1,602 per cent, at an annual compound rate
(inflation adjusted) of 157 per cent. Our market capitalisation has
increased from the £100m paid by Paternoster Stores to £1.4 billion.
Figure 15.2 shows profit before tax.

We are confident that our shareholders will continue to benefit from
their investment. The group still has substantial potential, which will be
realised by having professional managers operating good, solid businesses with focused customer bases. Our turnaround is in actuality an
evolution to continue to be a leader in the retail marketplace.

16 Aer Lingus

by David Kennedy,
Chief Executive, AER LINGUS

From the 1950s through to the late 1960s the development of the airline industry was particularly erratic – years of improving results would be followed by periods of setbacks and losses, and years of staff growth would be followed by lay-offs. Europe's airlines, including several of their flag carriers, suffered in this way, and in the US it was only the exceptional few which were able to maintain a steady course through the upswings and downswings. As recessions occurred, traffic growth would abate but airline capacity growth continued to increase. This inability of the industry to adapt production (i.e. seats) to demand (i.e. passengers) was at the heart of the cyclical problem.

The oil price surges in 1973 and 1979 seriously aggravated the problems of the airline industry, which never achieved the *consistent* return on capital employed that economic sense indicated.

Fortunately Aer Lingus, although not insulated from the cyclical problems of the industry, managed to avoid the stop/go experience of many other carriers. Aer Lingus operated in a relatively small market – travel to and from Ireland – and throughout the 1950s and 1960s it consistently dominated that market, both on the Atlantic (with its services to and from the United States) and in Europe (with its services to and from many British and Continental cities). In Europe our major competitor was BEA, which rightfully claimed that it was 'Europe's largest'. On the Atlantic, Aer Lingus fought for and maintained a dominant share of the US–Ireland traffic against the 'mighty twins', Pan Am and TWA, which throughout the 1960s and 1970s were the only US carriers on the North Atlantic.

However, the ability of Aer Lingus to outsell such major international carriers was no guarantee of good financial results. From the late 1960s surplus capacity (from the US 'supplementals') came on to the Atlantic route. They were the 'second arm' of the US strategic air carrier capacity and, as their strategic support became less needed elsewhere, the US authorities wanted to provide an opportunity for their 'supplementals' to prosper on the 'rich pickings' of the Atlantic.

In the consequent Atlantic battle of the 1970s there were many casualties among the US supplementals, but heavy losses were also experienced both by the European national carriers and the US scheduled airlines. Certain European carriers further aggravated the surplus capacity problem, e.g. Laker Airlines. Inevitably, as capacity grew, fares tumbled; also as fares tumbled, traffic grew, but balance between costs and revenue was elusive. In the flurry of politics and controversy which beset Atlantic air fares throughout the 1970s business prudence had but a small audience.

In retrospect the North Atlantic air transport market presented a fairly classic confrontation between established 'haves' fighting to 'hold on' and hungry 'have nots' fighting to gain a place. Both groups can behave in a fashion reminiscent of gladiatorial 'battles to the death'. Add to that conflict the 1973 explosion in oil prices and the second oil crisis in 1979, which between them increased fuel prices tenfold. By 1980 the once vaunted 'blue riband route' of civil aviation was flying a 'tattered ribbon'. In the words of such respected newspapers as the *New York Times* and the *The Times* of London, the North Atlantic had become a 'financial bloodbath'.

In the early 1970s Aer Lingus, seeing what was happening in the industry, realised that its own problem was not one merely of 'cyclical variances', nor one merely of sharing in the general problem experienced by all Atlantic carriers. Through dominating its markets and expanding prudently, it had avoided the worst of the 'stop-go' experiences of many others. The traditional Aer Lingus view was that the shorthaul and seasonal nature of our European network was inherently not economic or, at best, only marginally so, and would have to be supported by a profitable Atlantic operation. Now that the longhaul (Atlantic) operation was producing results that were even worse than those of the shorthaul division, the serious question to be addressed was whether there was any direction Aer Lingus could take towards prosperity.

Tight budgetary control had replaced the easier conditions of the 1960s. A people-orientation in service was being highlighted. But such approaches had failed to close the cost/revenue gap. With some courage a strategy of diversification was decided upon.

The first decision was that the experience and skills Aer Lingus had gained in the air transport industry should be marketed internationally so as to contribute to improved group results. As expressed at corporate level, the idea was to attract other business which would 'underpin' the airline's own travel business. A senior management reorganisation redeployed the necessary expertise so that this programme could receive sustained guidance and direction.

From a small base in international airline training considerable success attended an ambitious programme of selling the airline's aircraft-maintenance capacity, traffic handling, management, communications and computerisation skills to the airline industry worldwide. This activity could be seen as an 'organic' expansion into diversification. But the second approach to the airline's diversification target was more adventurous.

In 1973 Aer Lingus opened an 850-bedroom hotel – the London Tara – in our main airline destination. Other property diversifications were less successful at the time, but the acquisition of a stake in the then newly formed London-based Guinness Peat Group was followed by the joint creation of what is now known as the Shannon-based GPA Group. This group started in a small way as an aircraft broker but has now become spectacularly successful as a multinational supplier of leased aircraft to the world's airlines.

Another investment which delivered outstandingly good results was the Dunfey Hotels Corporation in New Hampshire. It was acquired in January 1976 from the Aetna Insurance Corporation of Hartford, Connecticut, after 2 years of intensive negotiation and examination of the hotel properties. For an equity of £370,000 Aer Lingus acquired the Dunfey Corporation, with fourteen leased and three managed hotels.

From the outset the Dunfey Hotels were a rewardingly good investment. At the time of acquisition the seventeen Dunfey hotels were largely situated in New England, but by 1987 most of the original hotels had been re-leased while twenty-eight others had been added, including the prestigious Omni chain. Ten years after the first step, our American hotel operation had grown to a chain of thirty-one new and classic hotels, largely trading under the Omni label, spread across twenty-three states of the USA, and a programme to franchise the Omni name and associated hotel management systems had been launched successfully. The investment had done more for Aer Lingus than had been expected, but still in the late 1980s there could be cause for reviewing the structure of our investment in an industry that manifested problems of slow growth in the US. Meanwhile Aer Lingus in 1987 acquired the UK-based Copthorne Hotel chain from British Caledonian to build on the outstanding success of its London Tara.

In mainland Europe Aer Lingus in 1979 acquired the Commodore Hotel in Paris and brought that hotel into profit, a task in which previous owners had failed. Also in that year Aer Lingus completed its buyout of Irish Helicopters, a company which, despite its name, had been wholly under UK control until Aer Lingus took its first stake in it. Aer Lingus was now able to profit directly from oil exploration activity in Irish waters.

As a result of its efforts, the airline returned to profit in 1976, having made a faster recovery from the first oil crisis and the problems of the North Atlantic route than had at first seemed possible. Profits expanded in the following years but the Group was then hit by the second oil shock in 1979–80, which was to lead to the worst financial crisis ever faced by the aviation industry, with massive losses being sustained by almost every airline worldwide.

We were no exception. In 1980–81 the Aer Lingus Group incurred the largest deficit in its history. Despite earnings from diversified activities, the major losses from air transport raised the prospect that the shareholders' equity would be lost within 2 years unless the fortunes of the Aer Lingus Group as a whole could be reversed dramatically. Debt as a percentage of total assets in 1981 was a staggering 88 per cent, while, at the same time, we were aware that substantial capital investment would be needed later in the decade to renew the airline's shorthaul fleet.

The profits from diversified activities were far ahead of the figures envisaged when that programme was inaugurated in 1972. But there was a confluence of problems on the airline side – the continued Atlantic problem, the international recession, Ireland's own economic problem of excessive inflation, and the Northern Ireland problem affecting inbound traffic. All these severely aggravated the underlying problems of the bulk of the Aer Lingus network – an extremely short high season and low (discounted) average fares. The fundamental question could not be avoided. Did the airline's basic structure now need *radical surgery*?

There was no doubting where the major problem lay – the Atlantic route. The US–Ireland market was even more difficult than the routes to such major European destinations as London. Throughout the 1970s we had analysed it again and again. The bitter conclusion was that the high seasonality, relatively thin volume, low business and high tourist traffic mix using low promotional fares made the route a particularly poor business prospect. The abandonment of Ireland by the two major US Atlantic carriers, Pan Am and TWA, confirmed this analysis. The twin terminals of Shannon and Dublin – both required for significant traffic reasons (apart from any considerations of regional policy) – exacerbated the problem.

As the oil crises pushed up fuel prices, the relatively fuel-thirsty Boeing 707s had become uneconomic and had been retired. We had acquired a third B747 in 1979 on a long-term lease/purchase arrangement. This third B747 enabled Aer Lingus to continue its dominance of the Ireland–US routes, but sadly the Montreal and Chicago destinations had been dropped from the network – their thinner and far too seasonal traffic in no way justified B747 service, whose low seat–mile cost came into its own by concentrating volumes on New York and Boston. (Alternative fleet strategies were studied minutely but their economics disqualified them as possible contenders.) It was clear that this rationalisation of fleet and routes undertaken would not suffice to achieve reasonable financial results.

Could the Atlantic route be sustained at all with a 1980–81 loss of £18m? Should the airline contract back to two B747s? On that question the analysis concluded that such a contraction would have very little effect on the problem. The major finding was that the Atlantic route had now reached the point that it *could no longer be justified on a commercial basis*.

An exhaustive study, which also encompassed the European routes, developed a 'Strategy for Survival'. We engaged US-based strategic consultants to validate or amend our conclusions. This exercise included a detailed study of Aer Lingus costs relative to those of our competitors.

The outcome was a formal submission to the Irish Government as shareholder. The 1981 consultants concluded, as other consultants had concluded in the past, that the airline was seriously undercapitalised, with a debt/equity ratio of almost 7/1. Given the nature of its commercial task, Aer Lingus could not sustain interest payments on the accumulated debt, a substantial part of which was due to high Atlantic losses through the 1970s. The efficiency of the airline was compared to those which operated on the much less seasonal US–London routes. The incidence of heavy promotional costs was studied for what in effect is a secondary destination relative to London or Paris. Economies of scale relative to competitors were tested and the financial penalty arising from the Irish twin terminals was quantified.

Following these studies and the consultants' report, the shareholder was advised that withdrawal from the Atlantic route, disposal of the Atlantic longhaul fleet, and major redundancy both in the US and Ireland would have to be faced unless further equity were provided. In addition, cost alleviation payments would be required to compensate for the unique cost penalties inherent in the operation of the Irish routes.

Government consideration of the Aer Lingus submission covered issues such as the effect on tourism and industrial development of the cessation of an Irish-owned Atlantic operation, with its attendant promotional expenditure in North America. The shareholder directed that the Atlantic route should be continued. New equity of IR£30m was to be provided (a sum less than half the amount already lost on the Atlantic routes). In addition, up to IR£15m was to be paid in staged cost alleviation payments.

The ball was now back with the airline management – to continue cost-cutting, to become increasingly aggressive in marketing and to further expand earnings from diversified activities. By 1986 increasingly intensive and imaginative cost-cutting, particularly on payroll and fuel but also on a wide range of other expenses, effectively reduced the cost base of the airline's air-transport activities by about IR£25m per annum. The Atlantic freighter service was withdrawn and subcontracted to an independent cargo airline in which Aer Lingus had bought a stake in 1980. Without compulsory redundancy, but as a result of redeployment, the diversified activities, early retirements and non-replacement, a reduction of 1,000 staff (or approximately 20 per cent) was achieved in the airline's own air transport operation.

The airline's computerisation talents were applied to new fields, of which a turnkey reservation system for a Middle East airline was an outstanding example. But it was also necessary to be increasingly active in computerising Aer Lingus's own marketing and sales areas, both in-house and in the retail travel trade sectors.

To expand the airline's earnings from sale of its engineering expertise, Airmotive Ireland, a stand alone (off airport) engine overhaul plant, was opened in 1981, attracting over 75 per cent of its business from airlines around the world. PARC, a personnel recruitment agency founded in the 1970s and previously concentrating on the supply of airline skills worldwide, now entered new fields. In 1982 PARC achieved the relative wonder for Irish enterprise of completing a contract with the Iraqi authorities for equipping and managing a major new referral hospital in

Baghdad. In 1986 PARC, through a subsidiary PARC CARE Limited, brought its hospital management expertise into the field of care for the elderly through the acquisition of a chain of nursing homes in the UK. In Tenerife extensive villa and apartment construction, combined with the opening of Hotel Santiago in November 1986, promised that the Aer Lingus site, which had been acquired in the mid-1970s and lain fallow until the early 1980s, would now produce a strong profit stream for the Group. Some seed investment in the exciting field of robotics was made in 1985 and by 1987 our Canadian robotics subsidiary was well exceeding our initial expectations. The ancillary activities of the airline prospered across almost their entire range.

But it was clear to management that, to consolidate a turnaround, fresh departures were also essential in the core business of air transport, the *raison d'être* of Aer Lingus. The focus of every service industry must be on the human dimension, the personal wants and needs of its customers. Standards of service campaigns had been executed in the past, but in 1983 we had the most thorough ever analysis of all the airline's marketing practices and performance standards. Marketing targets were redefined sector by sector. While the priority of the tourist market for future growth was reasserted, the need to cater for the business traveller specially was given a new highlight.

The Airline's 'Quality Quest' programme ensued. It required a major and personalised initiative on the part of Aer Lingus management, as well as its sustained commitment over many months, to galvanise the systemwide organisation to pursue the Quality Quest objectives. These were summarised as follows:

- clean, modern and attractive aircraft at all times
- timings and schedules fully geared to the customer's needs
- punctuality in operations that met the customer's expectations
- standards of service that were better than any competitor's, person to person, on the ground and in the air

While this programme was undertaken, Aer Lingus recognised a special problem on our thinner routes from Ireland to some UK provincial cities. Traffic had suffered from the decline in resident Irish populations, as well as from the general recession. Lower load factors were making it uneconomic to maintain suitable daily frequencies. In a complete reversal of the trend to larger and faster aircraft Aer Lingus acquired four Belfast-made 35-seater Shorts 360 aircraft and created a new subsidiary – Aer Lingus Commuter. The S360s began to serve Liverpool, Bristol, the East Midlands, Leeds/Bradford and Edinburgh. They also made improved frequencies possible on the domestic Dublin–Cork route.

The 1984–85 Annual Report of Aer Lingus noted gratifying results from the 'Commuter initiative' and from 'Quality Quest'. On a broad range of service elements passenger compliments had increased and adverse comments were well down. Improvements had been achieved in punctuality. A new Executive Class was introduced on European routes. The Atlantic Executive and First Class service was embellished. In 1985 an IATA survey of 80,000 Atlantic passengers rated Aer Lingus first or joint first under eighteen out of twenty-two service headings. In the same year our improving standards at our Dublin headquarters resulted in British Airways rating Aer Lingus as their top handler in Europe.

Of course, to realise their full potential, marketing initiatives must reach the pricing area. Here sophisticated new marketing techniques enabled us to restructure fares, giving compelling new low fares in several markets where demand justified and economics allowed. Aggressive promotion and marketing, together with refurbished standards, in time paid dividends. Air transport could report substantially improved results by 1985, but an indication that the wider industry still had problems was the withdrawal in the 1980–5 period not merely of the remaining US 'supplementals' but of two new US scheduled carriers from the Ireland–US routes. Both these airlines subsequently ceased all operations, but nevertheless by 1986 a third pair of US carriers ventured into the Ireland–US markets.

From the low-point losses of IR£11.4m in 1980–81, the Aer Lingus Group's financial results showed steady improvement. Losses fell to IR£1.7m in 1982–83, changing to profits of IR£8.5m the following year with subsequent yearly improvements until in mid-1987 the airline's fiftieth year celebrations culminated in a record net profit of IR£19.9m.

The previous year's Annual Report (1985–86) had this message from the Chairman:

In each of the past five years substantial profit improvement has been achieved, with the 1985/86 results exceeding all previous years by a substantial margin. To have obtained these results in a year of continued slackness in the demand for air transport, of intensified competition and of further pressure on costs, represents a strong achievement by management and employees throughout the Aer Lingus Group.

When profits from its diversified business were subtracted, the air-transport activity was still giving unsatisfactory returns. In a year of record profits air transport had generated 55 per cent of the group's operating profits but it had earned only 18 per cent of group profits after interest. But the airline scene was still changing in 1986: US traffic to Europe fell, fuel prices began to tumble, new competition arrived and Aer Lingus introduced lower promotional fares on the Atlantic and on Continental European routes. New low fare entrants on the Ireland–London routes found themselves undercut by Aer Lingus as a result of a sustained series of reductions in promotional fares, so that our marketing was based on the slogan 'No one flies you to London and back for less'. Throughout 1986 and 1987 traffic responded with record levels of growth and the airline's total marketing effort was a key factor in the significant rise in foreign visitors to Ireland in 1987.

Profits for the year 1987–88 (yet to be announced at the time of writing) are likely to exceed the previous year's record results by a substantial margin. Through our normal profit stream and through substantial capital profits arising from carefully chosen partial divestment of some ancillary activities, we have successfully addressed the problems of the Group balance sheet. In March 1987 the airline's debt/equity ratio stood at a relatively healthy 41/59 – a dramatic improvement on the frightening 88/12 ratio of 1981.

With this new balance sheet the airline has found it possible to begin the first phase of its European fleet replacement programme. In November 1987 we acquired two new Boeing 737–300 aircraft and placed orders for four more 737s of the 400 or 500 marque for delivery in early 1990. All these aircraft are being acquired without resort to our shareholder for additional equity.

Reflecting on what Aer Lingus has achieved from the low point of 1980–81, I am conscious of the tremendous commitment, resourcefulness and stamina of the airline's human resources. These characteristics were not only evident in the performance of management across the wide range of our activities, but they could also be seen in the airline's staff at all levels, particularly in the vital areas of personal service.

The recovery programme was founded on three supports: first, on a fundamental strategic analysis of the company's activities, its strengths and weaknesses, and on an identification of opportunities for new business development; secondly, on a marketing programme which recognised the realities of the increased competitiveness of the airline industry and which placed the appropriate emphasis on price and standard of service; thirdly, on a radical and imaginative campaign of cost-cutting which questions every expense item so that any middle-age spread in costs can be trimmed away, leaving a lean and agile frame well able to handle the opposition in the newly competitive conditions which we face.

On our forty-fifth birthday in 1981, Aer Lingus reported record losses and we were forced to admit to unease about our future. A measure of the turnaround achieved is that now, having passed our fiftieth birthday, it is with a substantial measure of confidence that the Aer Lingus Group faces the new challenges which lie ahead.

17 Grattan

by David Jones, Deputy Chairman and Managing Director, GRATTAN PLC

The mail-order industry enjoyed 25 years of continuous growth between the mid-1950s and the end of the 1970s, interrupted only by a postal strike in 1971. The growth started with the introduction of the 'approval' system – send for goods on approval and return them if you do not like them – and the improvement in the quality and branding of the merchandise offered in the glossy catalogues, which rapidly grew to 1,000 pages.

During the 1960s Grattan, although not the largest company in the industry, certainly had the reputation of being one of the best. It had high profits, a loyal agency base and an unsurpassed reputation for quality.

The 1960s were the 'fun' years in mail-order – business grew very rapidly, new agents were cheap to get, the labour force was low paid – so that any problems relating to higher volumes were simply solved by taking on more people. Computers had not really arrived – merchandise forecasting was done on the back of an envelope; agents' and customers' records were manually maintained, so that very little was known about the habits of individual purchasers; and, incidentally, profit margins were high!

The 1970s were far more difficult – wage rates soared, there was a Post Office strike and profit margins were eroded. This gave tremendous impetus for expenditure on computers and warehouse mechanisation. The marketing men carried on the 1960s philosophy of playing the numbers game, i.e. spend more on recruitment advertising in magazines and get more applications, offer all agents everything you sell, send out a new catalogue every 6 months and sit back and wait for the orders to come in.

Throughout the 25 years of growth the mail-order companies did not consider themselves part of high-street retailing and therefore looked only at other catalogue companies as their competition. Mail-order was about three things only – buying, despatching from warehouses and funding debtors. The industry was relatively untouched by the concept of marketing: in short, it had begun to lose touch with what the consumer really wanted and several decades of growth had led to a high degree of complacency.

During the years of growth the big selling advantages of catalogue mail-order were credit, commission and convenience, but at the end of the 1970s these traditional advantages were losing their appeal. Credit, for instance, was no longer the monoploy of the mail-order companies; the high-street was offering credit and the use of personal credit cards was growing. Commission was no longer a dominant factor, because the income per agent was dropping as the average number of customers per agent fell from sixteen in 1960 to around four in 1976. All catalogue mail-order companies found that they had a small percentage of their agents who were still 'running a business', but a much larger number of agents really only wanted a catalogue for their own family requirements. The convenience factor was still there but the mail-order industry had to make it easier for the home shopper to shop, as well as modernise its image.

Grattan, the mail-order success story of the 1960s, suffered in the late 1970s because of these changes in the style of the industry, but more so because of the complete lack of systems development within computers and warehouse development. A policy of increasing market share at any cost in the late 1970s led to a rapid increase in turnover, but the lack of adequate computer systems, an antiquated warehouse operation and the lack of bad-debt controls all but ruined the business.

Drastic action was needed, and in 1981 a new management team was recruited from a major competitor. David Jones, previously Managing Director of the British Mail Order company – a subsidiary of GUS, and the largest mail-order company in the UK – joined as Chief Executive, with John Whitmarsh, also an ex-Gus man, joining as Computer Director.

David Jones now takes up the story.

'GETTING CONTROL' OF GRATTAN

We recognised on the first day we arrived that we had a real problem. Grattan had almost 500,000 agents, and their accounting records were almost entirely maintained manually – the office systems were akin to those at Kays of Worcester where we worked in the 1960s. The computer systems were a shambles, with high expenditure on IBM and ICL machines, plus a multitude of mini-computers with little or no real commercial or financial benefits.

Our first objective therefore had to be to get control of the business, which was achieved within 12 months by the following means:

- The writing off of all the existing computer equipment and the installation of a large Amdahl mainframe computer
- The complete reprogramming of the agency, order-processing and warehousing systems
- The development of improved warehouse handling techniques in the existing four-storey warehouse at Bradford

The task of educating a very large company in new methods of operation and control was a daunting task, but made easier by the recognition of the Grattan employees that unless something was done quickly, we could not survive in a highly competitive retail environment.

The most difficult factor was the inevitable reduction in staffing levels which was essential as the new systems became operational. We had to concern ourselves with the welfare and job security of the majority of our employees but remember the tremendous loyalty of all the Grattan staff. Consequently the reduction in staffing levels were very largely achieved by voluntary redundancy on terms significantly more favourable than the statutory minimums.

Improving the operational efficiency of Grattan was perhaps the easiest task, because the new management team, with many years of mail-order experience behind it, knew fundamentally what had to be done. Recognising the problems in the mail-order industry and dealing with those was the real challenge.

'REVITALISING' GRATTAN

We could see that by the early 1980s catalogue mail-order was at a crossroads. It was perhaps not surprising that this was the case because the mail-order trade had experienced many years of very successful growth, and was therefore due for a rethink of its competitive strategy.

Grattan asked itself three questions:

- How can we make our methods of shopping even more convenient?
- How can we improve and update our merchandise offer and catalogue presentation?

• How can we use our vast database to work for us?

Convenience factor

Mail order was a convenient method of shopping, but what did convenience mean? It meant basically that people could look through a catalogue in their own home and have merchandise delivered to their own home to inspect.

We set out to retain these obvious advantages and to improve the method of ordering and the speed of delivery. We introduced telephone ordering and encouraged its use by opening our shop 7 days a week from 8.30am to 9.00pm. Agents can now ring Grattan, order their requirements, know immediately if they are in stock and, if items are out of stock (as inevitably a small number will be), either be able to order a similar item or find out exactly when the preferred item will be available. They can then decide whether they wish to wait for them or cancel.

We also invested in the modernisation of our warehousing systems, with the result that an agent ordering items on a Monday can expect delivery by Wednesday in the majority of cases, or Thursday. The old image of mail-order merchandise taking weeks to arrive has been totally overcome.

We also recognised that an increasing number of home shoppers did not want to run an agency. They did not want to sell merchandise to their neighbours or their friends at work, but simply wanted a catalogue for their own personal family use. We therefore introduced three new direct cataloguing trading names which were targeted to three specific groups – 'Look Again' to the younger age group, 'You & Yours' to the more traditional mail-order shopper and 'Streets of London' to the working woman who would find catalogue shopping more convenient because she did not have time to shop. In each of these companies the customer has a full range of merchandise without the onerous paperwork to complete. All she has to do is phone in her order, receive the goods, receive a monthly statement and pay in full or by instalments if she wishes to have a credit account.

Merchandise selection and presentation in catalogues

The mail-order industry used to advertise that the catalogue was 'A Departmental Store in your Home', but in the early 1980s departmental stores were not doing particularly well. The era of the specialist retailer had arrived – Next, Benetton, Chelsea Girl, Top Shop, Habitat, etc. All created environments which made shopping more attractive to the customers.

We therefore decided to divide our catalogue into shops and create catalogue pages that mirrored a shop window. We co-ordinated merchandise so that instead of simply selling a page of sweaters, we sold the sweaters, skirts, blouses, shoes, scarves and accessories all from the same catalogue illustration. We introduced brighter colours and allowed photographers and catalogue production designers the flexibility to experiment.

In addition, we looked at our suppliers and found that, in general, the clothing suppliers that we had been buying from basically supplied the mail-order trade – there was a different set of suppliers for the high-street. We began to introduce new suppliers who had already proved themselves as good high-street designers and manufacturers, and used their knowledge of merchandise trends to update the fashion offer in our catalogues. In doing this we changed a fundamental attitude of our buyers. Previously, they would have considered the competition as other mail-order companies. We encouraged them to consider that their competition was all other forms of retailing, of which the high-street was the most important part.

With the improved technology in printing we were able to finalise our merchandise selection much later, and therefore use the colour and design information that was available to the retail buyers. Even if we do miss out on a particular fashion trend, we do have a unique flexibility to fill a gap by producing a special leaflet or 'specialogue' to distribute to particular targeted groups.

Use of database

Mail-order companies have always collected information about the people they trade with, but this information was only used financially, e.g. we used it to reduce the number of unprofitable agents. We now began to keep detailed information of everything that was bought by our agents and customers. By analysing this information we were able to target new leaflets to those people most likely to buy from them. We were also able to use our vast database to select new names and addresses of people most likely to want to buy from one of our publications – for example, when we launched a new catalogue for outsize ladies' clothing, we initially sent it to people on our computer file who had previously ordered size 16 and above. We have targeted home electrical offers to people who have bought a video, but we have been careful not to target gardening leaflets to those people who live in flats.

Even now the use of database for marketing purposes in this way is in its infancy. The future developments are endless, particularly when one considers the offering of financial services by direct mail.

It is not an exaggeration to say that in the 1960s and 1970s our major selling offer was the main catalogue, which was distributed in January and July, and we all sat back and waited for the orders to roll in. Now that mail-order catalogues are in 5.8 per cent of homes in the country, we have to stimulate our business by a monthly communication, accompanied by new catalogues, new leaflets and special offers. We can no longer sit back and wait for things to happen: we have to go into our marketplace and make things happen.

An added bonus to the development of our vast database was created by the acquisition of Kaleidoscope in 1983, followed by Scotcade in 1985 and Aspect in 1987. These three well established direct-response mail-order businesses had flourished in the 1970s but declined in the early 1980s. By applying our technique of target marketing, backed up by our efficient order-taking and despatch facilities, we have been able to revitalise this very important part of the mail-order industry. We are now the market leaders in direct-response.

CONCLUSION

In 5 years Grattan was turned from a company that lost £5.5m in 1982 to one which produced a profit of £16m in 1986. Its first 5-year plan had been successfully achieved. Its second 5-year plan, which was developed in the middle of 1986, contained ideas relating to a new catalogue linked to a high-street name and the development of financial services by direct mail. It was fortunate that George Davies, who had achieved a similar dramatic turnaround in the fortunes of Next (previously Hepworths), had the same forward thinking ideas and philosophy. David Jones and George Davies merged their two companies in July 1986. *The Times* described it as a move 'that brought together two of the most successful retail brains of the 80's'.

The merger has been successful, which in itself is unusual in the retail trade at the moment! Early in 1987 Next Plc acquired the Combined English Stores and the Next Directory, a new-style home shopping catalogue, was launched in January 1988.

You will hear more from Davies and Jones.

18 La Vie Claire

by Marie-Pierre Vaur,
Public Relations Department, LA VIE CLAIRE

La Vie Claire is a company with an unusual background. Its founder, Henri-Charles Geffroy, had suffered severe lung damage from exposure to mustard gas during World War I. Although doctors had given up on him, he went on to cure himself, through using and eating totally natural products and cutting out all animal produce. Proud of his success, though thoroughly condemned by the medical profession, Geffroy chose to publicise his remarkable recovery through various media. It soon became clear that the public wanted to use the natural products he had praised so highly.

In 1952 therefore he set up a family-run co-operative, specialising in natural products and health foods. Thirty-six years later it is an international chain, with an annual turnover of 200 million francs and employing 200 staff in its different divisions.

But in June 1978, La Vie Claire faced liquidation. The unusual nature of the business and the shareholders' dedication to the founder's cause were to determine the various stages of La Vie Claire's recovery. Different food industry groups, including a large cheese manufacturer, were very interested when they heard of the problems facing a company that was the forefather of health food manufacture and a leader in its field. When the bankruptcy of La Vie Claire was announced, food industry groups strongly supported the judicial bodies and receivers, anticipating a decision on the takeover. But Bernard Tapie, a well-known French businessman, took a completely different approach. Rather than try to win over the different authorities now commissioned to manage the business, he chose instead to cultivate his relationship with the founder, Henri-Charles Geffroy.

At that moment Bernard Tapie demonstrated a stroke of genius. He is often cited as an example for his success in aiding the revival of companies in financial difficulty. Such companies have been successfully turned around thanks to Tapie's experience in the areas of finance, commerce and human relations.

Young Bernard Tapie (he is now only 43) came forward as La Vie Claire's saviour, with a dynamic and enthusiastic approach. Although suffering a huge financial deficit (48m francs in debt) the company was in a growth market and Bernard Tapie's team had great faith in it. The company had to its advantage a popular brand name, a corporate doctrine, a chain of shops, a fruit juice factory and the fact that it was the forerunner in its field, with a great deal of experience. All these factors in the company's favour inspired the people undertaking the recovery. They were determined not to let La Vie Claire go into liquidation.

AN UNUSUAL TURNAROUND

During its 10 years in business the Bernard Tapie Group has managed to climb to the top of the ladder in the production of health foods and industrial products. The Group's influential president gained popular credibility for the company by pursuing a strategy which included linking its image closely with sport.

In 1983 Bernard Tapie bought one of the best known sailing ships in the world (the ship, with four masts each measuring 72 metres, had belonged to the yachtsman Alan Colas, who was lost at sea). Tapie used it to break several records for crossing the Atlantic. In 1984 he set up a team of cyclists including Bernard Hinault, one of the most famous racing cyclists of the 1970s. In 1985 and 1986 the team won the Tour de France. Finally, in 1986 Tapie revived Marseilles' famous 'Olympic' football team, which until then had been completely disorganised, and led it to the final of the French cup.

Bernard Tapie has become well known in sporting circles and his popularity and success led inevitably to media coverage. He became a television director by leading a new broadcast devoted to unemployed people.

La Vie Claire is one of the first well-known companies that Bernard Tapie has turned around. His policy, which came into force shortly after Terraillon presented the company's assets and liabilities, was the starting point for a diversified holding company which was formed under a collective name, using Bernard Tapie's assets. The holding company today is divided into several equal divisions: food products, household and weighing equipment, batteries and other sidelines such as audio-visual equipment and fashion goods.

SANCTION FOR RESCUE

On the basis of a strong relationship with the founder of La Vie Claire, Bernard Tapie launched a plan of action designed to convince even the most suspicious supporters of the founder's family. An initial shareholders' meeting gave Bernard Tapie the authority to raise capital of 3m to 9m francs.

Henri-Charles Geffroy then presented Bernard Tapie as his successor. Tapie reassured the shareholders and discussed the part the founder's family was to play in the running of the company. A judicial administrator was selected ready for the court hearing.

The receiver pressed for the liquidation of the company to reimburse the shareholders, but Bernard Tapie took a different approach by showing his faith in the company. He was confident of the recovery and urgently requested the support of the shareholders. In March 1982, 90 per cent of the unsecured creditors voted in favour of Bernard Tapie's revival of La Vie Claire, and his proposal was sanctioned by the tribunal.

Secured creditors, as usual, had to be paid back within 3 years and the unsecured creditors had to be repaid over 8 years (four instalments of 10 per cent and four of 15 per cent). So far all the agreed payments have been made. In other words, 6 years after Bernard Tapie's turnaround of La Vie Claire, over 17m francs have already been repaid and the remainder will be paid over the next 3 years.

FACTORS CONTRIBUTING TO THE SUCCESSFUL RECOVERY

A company with a famous brand name, a corporate doctrine and a great deal of experience was certain to regain its successful position. However, the general public, who saw Bernard Tapie as a successful businessman, feared that his intervention would destroy the traditional image of La Vie Claire. It did not.

Among the first initiatives taken in favour of the brand's image was to emphasise quality standards. To this end an analysis and control laboratory, equipped with precision equipment, was set up.

Bernard Tapie broke the mould with a change in approach. Traditionally La Vie Claire had always opposed official procedures. The company had retained its competitive edge by systematically attacking the policies of different establishments and authorities in the country, such as doctors, pharmacists and manufacturers. Bernard Tapie set out to re-establish relations with these groups, presenting himself as a precursor of a new way of life and a new healthy diet to help prevent illness.

La Vie Claire is no longer known for engaging in political wrangles. Today the company markets itself as the doctor's ally, its job being to sell healthy products to the consumer. In pursuance of this aim, Dr Jean Duby, a sports doctor well-known in motor racing and football circles, was invited to maintain communication between the medical profession and La Vie Claire. Furthermore, during the last few years La Vie Claire has sponsored a tennis tournament for doctors, physiotherapists and nurses.

THE RESULTS OF TAPIE'S POLICY

The healing of rifts and an increase in publicity were undoubtedly the initial consequences of Bernard Tapie's policy. Previously, La Vie Claire's customers had been mostly people who were dissatisfied with ordinary medicines and had turned to natural remedies to cure their complaints. However, the new commercial attitude of the directors, which was to create a new image for the company, new standards for the products and a new colour scheme for the shops, resulted in La Vie Claire attracting a clientele that was younger, more active and free from preconceived ideas.

Bernard Tapie immediately boosted the commercial initiatives of La Vie Claire. He was always in the public eye and enjoyed a lot of media coverage. His public behaviour attracted many young people who showed a growing interest in the range of his activities.

Further initiatives included the development of certain product lines hitherto unthought of in the company. For example, in order to respond to the demands of the new consumers, La Vie Claire produced pre-cooked meals, dairy products, food supplements, goods for sportsmen and beauty products. The growth of the company's turnover had depended on the creation or buying up of small companies whose products La Vie Claire had used directly. In spite of everything, growth objectives were deliberately restricted so that the recovery plan was self-financing (in France 90 per cent of firms who embark on the road to recovery go bankrupt again).

During the summer, managers always used to close their shops for a month but following an awareness campaign conducted throughout the La Vie Claire chain the company has regained around 50 per cent of turnover during July and August. Today more than half of La Vie Claire shops are kept open throughout the summer.

Marketing initiatives also included the renovation and development of the chain of shops and the development of a previously unexploited export market in Great Britain, Belgium, Luxembourg and Japan. La Vie Claire's presence in these countries has been strengthened by the opening of shops. There is even a special agreement with Great Britain; Booker, a large English food company, bought up 38 per cent of La Vie Claire's shares and so became the second largest shareholder in the company after Bernard Tapie himself. The economic agreement between the two companies will inevitably lead to the cross distribution of goods in the near future: La Vie Claire will distribute Booker products in France and Booker will sell La Vie Claire products in its Holland and Barrett chain stores in Britain.

THE CHALLENGE FOR THE FUTURE

Bernard Tapie believes first that La Vie Claire's future lies in the development of retail outlets; he is hoping for 600 outlets for La Vie Claire and 100 for L'Herbier de Provence, the special brand name for their beauty products. Then he plans to penetrate such markets as the medical profession which had previously been hostile to La Vie Claire.

A number of small companies bought up several years ago should contribute to La Vie Claire's economic development. Each is a specialist in its field, such as the manufacture and distribution of beauty products and

the treatment and distribution of biological products through the traditional network of health-food shops.

In the near future these policies will allow La Vie Claire to expand
through a varied distribution network: with its own chain stores, stores
within large and small department stores, shelf space in health-food shops,
mail order and possibly contracts with larger groups of companies. It is not
unrealistic, therefore, to predict that La Vie Claire will double its turnover
in 3 years.

CONCLUSION

Henri-Charles Geffroy was an innovator. Long before it became fashionable, he had predicted that one day consumers would turn against processed and treated foodstuffs. He was, in effect, the French initiator of a
movement which has such a great following today. Perhaps one of La Vie
Claire's greatest regrets is that France decided to wait and learn from
America's experience before going into the distribution of natural food
products.

The founder of La Vie Claire had hoped that the sale of his products
would be part of a great reform in eating habits. Convinced that vegetarian-
ism was the only diet capable of preserving health, he completely banned
animal products, dairy products, eggs and honey from his shops. The
rejection of these products (which was later relaxed by Bernard Tapie) at
the time caused a lot of conflict with different industries. Today, in response
to public demand, La Vie Claire sells the products that Geffroy banned,
without compromising the quality necessary for the consumer's health.

The small co-operative of 1952 is a long way from the current position of
the company. La Vie Claire today has a network of more than 300
specialised shops throughout France and 1,500 products, including dry
goods, fresh fruit and vegetables, bread, special oils, whole cereals, hygiene
products, special products for sportsmen, dairy produce, cheeses, eggs and
soya products. In fact, La Vie Claire produces everything necessary for the
healthy consumer to maintain and improve his way of life.

19 Lucas

by Sir Godfrey Messervy,
Chairman and Chief Executive, 1980–7, Lucas

BACKGROUND

In 1981 Lucas made a loss for the first time in its 100-year history. Lucas was not of course alone in this experience. Between 1980 and 1982 most manufacturing companies in the UK went through a very bad patch. Under the three-way squeeze of rapid inflation, high interest rates and a hard pound sterling, most firms lost business to foreign competitors both in the UK and abroad. Nonetheless, when all extenuating circumstances had been taken into account, we in Lucas still had to face an unpalatable truth. Our performance relative to that of some competitors had become uncompetitive, and there was no quick and painless remedy available.

Historically Lucas was a supplier of a wide range of electrical systems and components to the British motor industry. Up to 1914 it specialised in headlamps and dynamos, and between the wars it added ignition, batteries, diesel fuel injection and braking equipment to its product portfolio. The post-war expansion of the British motor industry, however, saw Lucas rise to the front rank of systems and component suppliers. During the 1960s UK vehicle production peaked at just over 2 million units a year and held steady around that level until the early 1970s. Between 1973 and 1982, however, production fell by around 50 per cent, due largely to the near-collapse of British Leyland. The severe cyclical recession which began in 1979 merely sharpened this downward trend. As a result, during the late 1970s Lucas automotive companies experienced a serious loss of business in their UK markets and in 1981, after 3 years of declining financial performance, the Group went into the red (Table 19.1).

TABLE 19.1 *Lucas Industries plc Performance indicators, 1979–86*

	1979	1980	1981	1982	1983	1984	1985	1986
Total sales (£m)	1,072	1,196	1,186	1,220	1,217	1,397	1,499	1,620
Operating profit (£m)	70.7	53.2	5.0	35.3	20.1	47.9	67.7	110.5
Profit/(loss) before tax (£m)	70.7	41.0	(21.4)	20.2	2.1	32.6	57.8	95.2
Total capital employed (£m)	460	500	475	454	462	477	453	533
Profit before tax as % of capital employed	15.3	8.2	(4.5)	4.4	0.5	6.8	12.8	17.9

THE STRATEGIC RESPONSE

Fortunately our strategic response did not have to be devised from scratch. Since the late 1950s we had been building up our penetration of major automotive markets outside the UK by direct investment in manufacturing facilities in Germany, France, Spain, the United States, South America, the Far East and elsewhere.

This strategy of reducing our dependence on the UK automotive market was complemented by a parallel development, largely by acquisition, of our non-automotive interests. These interests were represented by Lucas Aerospace and a group of electronics companies which subsequently became Lucas Industrial Systems. Nevertheless the recession underlined the need for a fundamental reappraisal of Lucas's objectives and strategy. The strategic goals we adopted – and have been vigorously pursuing – represent a transformation of our business.

IMPLEMENTING THE STRATEGY

First objective

Our first objective was to reduce our UK resources to match the current and anticipated levels of automotive business, discontinuing activities with inadequate current and potential returns on capital. Our approach to the selection and development of 'winners', which we are rigorously applying to all our businesses throughout the Group, automotive and non-automotive alike, is aimed at the achievement of full international competitiveness. Every one of our business units is required to compare its performance with its best international competitor, identify any shortcomings and specify in detail how it intends to close any perceived performance gap in the shortest possible time. The resulting plan, called a Competitiveness Achievement Plan, or CAP, must be credible in its targets and affordable in terms of the resources it requires. If it is, then the CAP is approved and fully supported with the necessary manpower and financial resources. But those business units which, even with central help, cannot produce an acceptable CAP are earmarked for disposal, and many units have been closed or sold over the past 2 or 3 years.

Within Lucas Electrical, where a great deal of rationalisation has taken place, a relatively early decision (1984) was to withdraw from our loss-making French venture, Ducellier. Since then we have announced the closure of the main Great King Street factory in Birmingham and several other businesses in the Birmingham area, our withdrawal from both the electric vehicle systems and volume instrumentation businesses, and the sale of our vehicle lighting division to Fausto Carello SpA, our related company in Italy.

Another area of rationalisation is Lucas CAV in the UK where, in response to a sharp decline in the demand for tractors and commercial vehicles, a programme was introduced to reduce costs by rationalising both the product range and manufacturing capacity – significantly reducing the number of manufacturing sites. The closure of the CAV factory at Finchley was the latest change, announced in April 1987, and the production of fuel-injection equipment for automotive diesel engines is now concentrated on only two sites, at Gillingham in Kent and Sudbury in Suffolk.

The drive for full international competitiveness embodied in the CAPs developed at business unit level has in fact ensured that no part of Lucas Industries, however profitable it may be, has remained untouched. Lucas Girling, for example, has concentrated all its automotive braking businesses in the UK on two sites in South Wales, while Lucas Aerospace has been steadily pursuing a programme of cost-cutting in all its factories. This process has inevitably been painful both for Lucas and for the employees who have lost their jobs. Between 1980 and the first half of 1987, the company spent over £200m in reorganisation and redundancy and over the same period its total employment base in the UK fell by about 25,000 – well over one third. Nevertheless the action we have taken – and will continue to take in pursuit of full international competitiveness – is essential to our longer term prosperity.

Second objective

The fact that most of our rationalisation programme has been directed at our automotive businesses in the UK does not imply a strategic withdrawal from the automotive sector itself. On the contrary, our second but equally important objective was to develop our position as a major supplier of higher added value systems and components to the world automotive industry. Achieving this objective requires a continuing commitment to a high level of spending on Research and Development. In Lucas this expenditure has traditionally represented around 6 per cent of total sales income, a level of commitment which was maintained even during the darkest days of the recession.

The results are now showing through in the form of leading-edge technology products that are winning major international contracts. In braking equipment, for example, Lucas Girling's position as a leading European supplier has recently been confirmed by the successful launch of its anti-lock braking systems for high-volume, front-wheel-drive motor cars. Over half the cars in Japan are fitted with braking equipment made by Lucas Girling's licensees, and all major licence agreements have recently been renewed. Similarly, the recent launch of a new Lucas petrol injector underlines the strength of our product technology in the growing international market for engine management systems.

Third objective

Our third objective was to build up our successful aerospace business, which is already one of the largest suppliers of aerospace equipment in Europe.

Over the past few years we have won major contracts on international aerospace projects, such as the Airbus Industry A320, through a combination of leading-edge product technology and collaborative marketing with European and/or American partners. More recently, we have achieved a step-change in our already increasing penetration of the North

American aerospace market, which represents 80 per cent of the free world aerospace market, through the acquisition in 1987 of Western Gear Corporation, a company based in California and North Dakota. Western Gear's product range complements that of Lucas Aerospace, while its customer base spans all the major civil and military prime contractors in the USA. Earlier the same year we acquired two smaller businesses in the US aerospace industry – AUL Instruments, a defence electronics company, and Weinschel Engineering, a microwave supplier. These acquisitions have taken the total aerospace sales by our businesses in the USA to over $260m.

Simultaneously we have further strengthened our European base by acquiring Air Equipment and taking a 20 per cent stake in Messier Hispano Bugatti. Lucas now has an equity investment in European aerospace and defence businesses whose total sales exceed £300m.

Fourth objective

Our fourth objective is to add, by development and acquisition, to the range of systems and components supplied by our industrial division, to provide a range of quality products for targeted growth sectors.

About half our industrial systems business is in North America, and in 1987 we increased our penetration by acquiring Schaevitz, a leading US manufacturer of sensors and transducers. Schaevitz is a world leader in this rapidly growing high-technology market, with a good customer base in both North America and Western Europe.

The progress we have made in implementing our strategy is illustrated by Table 19.2.

TABLE 19.2 *Sectoral share of total group sales (%)*

	1980	1987
Automotive	82	63
Aerospace	13	27
Industrial	5	10

The sectoral composition of group sales will continue to change in favour of our aerospace and industrial businesses as we achieve a better alignment between our assets and our growth markets. Although the proportion of group turnover which is derived from the automotive sector is still large, the *quality* of these earnings is steadily improving, reflecting the growing importance of our markets and sales outside the UK, particularly in the EEC.

PEOPLE AND PRODUCTIVITY

In reassessing our competitiveness within Lucas our strategic analysis emphasised, more than any other single factor, the need to improve our manufacturing performance to match the best in the world. Lucas's manufacturing systems were originally designed to make low variety products in high volumes. In the market conditions of the 1950s and 1960s, these systems were very effective, but over the years they were modified incrementally, resulting in excessive numbers of indirect support staff, unduly complex control systems, and high and therefore costly stock levels, often with poor responsiveness to the changing needs of the marketplace.

Since the late 1970s there has been a clear trend in favour of higher variety products which we have been obliged to manufacture in variable but generally lower volumes. The only effective response to this trend is a fundamental redesign of the total manufacturing system. The key to effectiveness in manufacturing is the integration of new technology – modern machine tools and computers – with methodology. By applying a system engineering approach we have in recent years been progressively redesigning our factories on the basis of self-contained manufacturing cells, and introducing Japanese-style 'Just-in-Time' control systems. This process is by no means complete, but the results today have been very encouraging. In factories which have been restructured along these lines we have:

- improved the quality of the final product

- improved productivity by between 30 and 50 per cent

- reduced lead times by around 60 per cent

- reduced our stock levels by about 50 per cent

- achieved drastic reductions in indirect labour

and, no less important,

- equipped the direct labour force with a much broader and more flexible range of skills

Many of these improvements have been achieved with quite modest capital costs. Much more important has been our investment of time and expertise in designing and introducing new and much more flexible structures for jobs. These changes, however, would not have been achieved without a far-reaching programme of training and retraining Lucas managers, supervisors and craftsmen to equip them with the skills they need to operate the new manufacturing systems.

Training is in fact a major agent of change in Lucas. Like Research and Development, it is a vital investment in our future competitiveness, and is currently running at some £40m (2½ per cent of our total sales income) each year.

DEVELOPING A NEW MANAGEMENT STYLE

These changes add up to a fundamental break with the traditional corporate culture of Lucas, and yet they have been initiated, accepted and implemented by managers who for the most part have themselves been strongly influenced by the same culture over many years of service. New blood has certainly been introduced and we shall continue to recruit talented people from outside when the demands of a job cannot be met by internal promotion. But the turnaround in the performance and prospects of Lucas since the early 1980s essentially reflects the efforts of those who, having spent their formative years of service in a wholly different era, realised that they had to 'raise their game' if the company was to survive. This, in most cases, they did and the results are now showing through in the company's improving performance (see Table 19.1).

This raises the final and most fundamental lesson derived from recent experience, not just in Lucas but in most other organisations. Clearly there must be strong strategic leadership from the top so that people down the line have a clear sense of direction and purpose. But the real gains from cultural change come from the bottom up – from managers, supervisors and shopfloor workers in factories and business units. It shows most clearly when employees at this level take their own initiatives to achieve improved performance in some aspect of their business without waiting for instructions from above. It emerges in the form of a new willingness on the part of people throughout the organisation to take risks and raise their sights to achieve more demanding targets instead of simply 'playing it safe'.

There is of course no magic formula which will create this change in behaviour and it is to be regretted that so often it only begins to emerge in adversity. Nevertheless, for British industry as a whole to once again become and remain a major force in the world markets, our large companies need to be managed and staffed by people who make the right things happen.

20 Solaglas

by Alan Matchett, Planning and Marketing Director, SOLAGLAS LTD

Solaglas will be an unfamiliar name to many people, although it is the UK's biggest glass and glazing group, with a UK turnover in 1987–8 of £210m and 4,500 employees. It is the country's biggest producer of laminated and toughened safety glass, the biggest mirror manufacturer, and the biggest autoglass replacement company. It has more branches distributing glass and providing glazing than any other company. Solaglas is the new name for many long-established glass and glazing companies, which followed the acquisition by Solaglas International of Doulton Glass Industries from the Pearson group in 1982, and Windshields from the Ring Group and the independent James Clark & Eaton in 1983. The name Solaglas was introduced in October 1984 as one element in the unification and turnaround of these businesses.

Before their acquisition by Solaglas International, Doulton Glass Industries (DGI) and James Clark & Eaton (JCE) had problems. DGI was just one of several unrelated businesses forming Doulton & Co. Ltd, itself part of the Pearson Group. From profits of £3.8m in 1979 the business lost and wrote off £5.9m in 1981, caused by trading difficulties and write-offs associated with the disposal of its Cold Shield and other home improvement businesses. Morale in other parts of DGI was low, as traditional activities had been relatively neglected whilst the company had been expanding its double glazing and other home-improvement activities.

Disposal had also hit JCE. The company was the largest independent glass and glazing company in the country still family controlled and directed. In order to serve the expanding processed markets, the company had acquired a major production facility at Bracknell but various trading difficulties forced it to close this facility in 1982, with substantial redundancies. From a peak of 1,900 employees the company cut back to 1,000. Rationalisation costs of £1m created a severe strain on this privately funded business. The company was bought in December 1983, thus creating with DGI the national coverage that both had sought but had not been able to complete.

In 1983 Windshields Ltd was also acquired. Windshields was a specialist windscreen replacement fixing company, and was seen by Solaglas International as a strategic acquisition to complement the replacement autoglass business of DGI, which was called Autoglass. The acquisition was seen as having a major synergistic benefit. Whereas conventional synergy talks about $2 + 2 = 5$, the company was thinking in terms of $2 + 2 = 10$.

At the time of their acquisition, DGI and JCE were very different organisations in the way in which the businesses were operated and managed, and similarly Autoglass and Windshields, despite each serving the same specialist market. DGI had been highly decentralised. At the time of acquisition the business operated under forty-five different trading names, usually the retained trading names of the businesses acquired by Doulton & Co. Ltd. The six operating divisions conducted their activities largely independently of each other. Local companies could and did compete with each other for business. While many people recognised the problems of overlap created by such competition, they failed to recognise or address the much more severe problems of 'underlap' (failures to serve some customer needs, market segments and geographic areas effectively). Very little was done, apart from the colour of vehicles and some common literature, to present a unified face and promise to customers and potential customers. Crudely put, each branch 'did its own thing', and the company failed to exploit its position as market leader effectively.

The contrasts with JCE could hardly have been greater. Although JCE had similarly grown by acquisition, it had adopted a policy of changing the name of all acquired businesses. Whereas DGI frequently retained the title of managing director at individual locations, JCE called people branch managers. Accounts, systems support and purchasing were handled centrally at JCE; at DGI, accounting was largely decentralised and document layout and details were very different between regions. Sales people at JCE came under divisional control whereas DGI was largely branch-based. JCE was a more controlled and directed business than DGI, but of course paid a price in terms of losing some of the creative energy that DGI had with its many local managers trying to expand what they saw as their own business.

This same centralised versus decentralised style was echoed in the automotive glass replacement business. Autoglass, although set up to be a new, co-ordinated activity, was largely decentralised in practice, as operational control and drive from the centre was limited. Autoglass frequently shared sites with general glazing branches, and attitudes were local rather than national. Windshields was national in outlook and centralised in control. It believed that effective service to a mobile customer group demanded common standards everywhere. Insurance company recommendation was seen as highly desirable in projecting the right image and in securing business, and this recommendation could only be earned if the company was seen to be centrally disciplined and controlled. To make this a reality, Windshields had very early on been a user of a national freefone number in order to monitor and direct the activities of branches in responding to emergency calls.

So this was the picture at the beginning of 1984. Three different businesses had been acquired, with very different histories, cultures and ways of doing things. Trading profitability was negligible, and employees were uncertain about job security. The upside potential was, however, considerable. The new Group was clearly the biggest company in the business, it had in its constituent businesses long and close relations with many customers, it had a large and skilled workforce and it had new owners who were committed to the glass industry.

Given the understandable uncertainty that surrounded employees and customers, it was felt that change should be limited in the immediate aftermath of the acquisitions, although some organisational change was implemented right away. Three operating divisions were established – Glass, Safety Glass and Automotive – with managing directors reporting to the Group MD. Because DGI and JCE had had limited branch overlap, the amount of change in responsibility for branches was very small. Autoglass and Windshields experienced more impact, as it was recognised that a single cohesive entity was essential to serve the customer effectively. A new company called Autoglass Windshields was formed, a new livery developed and all vehicles, signs and stationery were changed. Some redundancies arose from the merger, but Autoglass Windshields immediately became much stronger than either operation had been alone, benefiting from more widespread coverage and better access to finance to speed up further expansion of the business.

Although the merging of the names Autoglass and Windshields was simple and effective, the same opportunity was not available for DGI and JCE. A condition of the sale was that the Doulton name had to be dropped within 3 years, and anyway the Doulton Glass Industries name was not used or known by customers, who continued to use local names. Research was undertaken to see which, if any, of the available names was known and respected throughout the industry. Not surprisingly all the names were little known outside their own local region, and even within a region their reputations were very mixed.

A common name was considered desirable to help the unification of the acquired businesses. Various options were researched, and the one judged to be most acceptable was the parent name Solaglas. However, given the need to maintain customer and employee loyalty and confidence, it was decided to prefix traditional names with the word Solaglas rather than to drop them right away. Thus James Clark & Eaton became Solaglas Clark Eaton, Simon Kalson became Solaglas Kalson and so on.

The next stage was to develop the communication package. Pentagram, the design group, was called in to develop an appropriate logotype and corporate identity to cover all the Group activities other than the distribution and fixing activities of the Automotive Division. As an indication of what needed to be done, nearly 2,000 variations of forms had to be brought into a common design style. A new corporate brochure summarising the Group's extensive range of products and services was developed, and advertising was undertaken to support the name change to specifiers and customers, and to introduce the new corporate slogan: 'Solaglas – Glass with the world's best service behind it'. The whole package was presented in a press launch in October 1984, and roadshows were held throughout the Group to explain the reason for the new name.

Concurrently the management team was working on the development of a Group Mission Statement. This was an explicit summary of what the Group sought to be, and identified actions necessary to make the Mission target achievable. This statement was then presented to and discussed throughout the Group, so that people were aware of the Group's objectives and what needed to be done. The need to improve standards was explicitly recognised. Significant investment was therefore made to improve manufacturing facilities and to improve services, following the squeeze on the businesses caused by their problems before acquisition.

As the businesses bedded down together during 1984, it became obvious that there were still problems. Although the Group now had a Mission and some unifying elements, such as the corporate identity programme, it was clear that the unification was only skin deep. The names on buildings and vehicles might be uniform, but the attitudes and behaviour of many people still tended to reflect the past. People still talked about 'them and us' when referring to DGI and JCE, and vice-versa. Traditional rivalry – for example between Coventry (DGI) and London (JCE) – was slow to fade, not because of ill-will or malice, but simply because many people had not recognised the opportunities now available to the Group from mutual help and shared experience.

It was also clear that there were great inconsistencies in performance around the operating locations, but no clear understanding of why this was so. Management information systems on branch performance were inadequate to identify key differences that could be used to enhance other branches' performance. A Group-wide study was therefore undertaken by management consultants McKinsey, working with Group employees, to identify what really made the difference in performance. A best-practice programme was then developed to spread good ideas and working procedures. Initially paired branch analyses were undertaken to contrast a good branch with an under-performer. Later the process was simplified so that effort could be concentrated on the under-performers – creating a ratchet effect whereby the bottom branches were moved up, exposing new branches for assessment and help in their turn.

In the Glass Division a league table of performance was drawn up and reported against each month. Branches could see their position and performance relative to those branches immediately above and below them, so that they could directly assess what they had to do to rise further up the rankings. At the end of the first year special ties or scarves were given to all employees at winning locations, draws were held for other prizes and a special winners' weekend was held in London.

The McKinsey study also confirmed the fact that the three operating divisions were not particularly well structured to meet the evolving needs of the marketplace. Competition was becoming increasingly severe from specialist companies, whereas with limited exceptions the Group was not well focused. The Group MD, Ronnie Lamb, therefore developed an outline restructuring of the organisation, and presented it to senior managers in September 1985. The organisational change envisaged was not simply concerned with structural change, although this was important, but also strategic and operational changes.

The organisational change was presented under a unifying theme which continues to be the focus of the Group's attitude and commitment: 'Being First'. The theme was not stated in the aspirational terms 'Become First' or 'Be First', because the company was already leader in the industry. 'Being First' represented the state of mind necessary to stay leader – the excitement and challenge of being No. 1, staying No. 1, and setting higher standards for others to follow.

The theme, or vision, was expressed in further detail to embrace strategic objectives, organisation structure and focus, and operational behaviour . . .

'the way we do things round here'. Against this vision, it was clear that there would need to be a change in focus within the operating businesses in order to serve customers better and to improve the company cost structure. An outline restructuring into five divisions was presented, and task-forces established to see whether the proposed restructure was likely to prove effective.

After the detailed task-force reviews, the new divisional structure of five operating divisions was implemented in April 1986. In addition to the changes in the operating divisions, it was also recognised that change was needed in the role of the Group head office. The requirement was for the head office both to be more directive as to where the Group should go, and to be more of a service to operating divisions until such time as they were strong enough to stand on their own. The head-office team was strengthened, but in due course numbers will be reduced, with people working in the operating divisions wherever possible.

These changes to the divisions and head office were communicated Group-wide via roadshows and local meetings. The messages of the roadshow were simple: focus is essential, superior customer service is essential, and superior customer service needs the personal commitment of everybody to be the best in his/her particular activity.

As indicated earlier, the Being First theme originally outlined in September 1985 has become a major unifying programme for the Group. At a senior management conference glass pyramids – the Being First symbol – were given out with instructions to pass them on to individuals or groups for outstanding contributions towards customer service or Group development. Having awarded a pyramid, the manager then receives a new one ready to award exceptional merit again. Publicity for winners is given in the Group newspaper, and will be used in future videos planned to communicate ongoing performance to all employees.

The turnaround in the company's fortunes is already visible, but there is still considerable room for improvement in almost all aspects of service and performance. Market share has increased in almost all market segments; in windscreen replacement, for example, current market share is running at twice the level that the separate businesses enjoyed before acquisition. Sales in the last financial year were 35 per cent ahead of the previous year and, more importantly, the business is now healthily profitable. Return on net assets has improved to 25 per cent, despite the investment costs of developing two new divisions.

In the past Solaglas has been predominantly a trade-orientated business. The opportunity, now being pursued, is to build a domestic business too.

The new Home Improvement Division is one manifestation of this, so is the new domestic replacement glazing service with insurance company recommendation, which has now gone national.

In April 1987 the logical next step in the corporate identity was taken, with most of the traditional company names being dropped. The company is now simply Solaglas for most of its activities and Autoglass for its windscreen-fixing business.

The basic themes and objectives of the Group are simply expressed: the customer must be given the best possible service; the individual must be respected; and excellence and superior performance must be pursued. These objectives are by no means unique to Solaglas – they are the basic themes of many service companies who are, or who strive to be, the best in their field. The turnaround already evident is only the start of the commitment to Being First.

INDEX

The Mercury titles on the pages that follow may also be of interest. All Mercury books are available from booksellers or, in case of difficulty, from:

Mercury Books
W.H. Allen & Co. Plc
44 Hill Street
London W1X 8LB

Further details and the complete catalogue of Mercury business books are also available from the above address.

BREAKTHROUGHS!

How leadership and drive created commercial innovations that swept the world.

By P. Ranganath Nayak and John M. Ketteringham and based on an international study of innovation by Arthur D. Little Inc.

Breakthroughs! testifies to the power that believing in one's dreams can give us. It is also a riveting study of people who, by finding big needs and little openings and filling them, made world-sweeping commercial breakthroughs that have in some way touched the lives of most of us. Behind each of these stories is a remarkable account of impossible visions made possible by human endeavour. It examines the creativity and ingenuity, determination and the special skills, the politics and perceptions that were required to open the way to new processes and products that have changed the way millions of us do things.

This book explodes the myths promoted elsewhere that success depends on corporate culture, intra- or entrepreneurship, market pull, or other such simple explanations. Instead it reveals a fascinating, far more subtle process for success that links such disparate ventures as 3M's little yellow self-stick notes, VCRs, EMI's CT scanners, microwave ovens, and the Sony Walkman to name a few. The authors study a deeper level of the success pattern: how early steps were taken; the key transition from concept to action; what worked and what didn't; why the competition lost out, and more. We learn the what, why and how of these breakthroughs from idea to development to domination – and even creation – of world markets. And behind it all, we meet the creative, driven individuals who never gave up until they realised their dreams, and we learn about the often circuitous paths they had to take to achieve those dreams.

Everyone who is mesmerised by innovation and how to manage it successfully will be engrossed by this revealing picture of the climate that lets good ideas break through every barrier to become reality.

ISBN 1–85251–075–7   £14.95

WHO CARES WINS

How to unlock the hidden potential in people at work . . . and turn ordinary companies into winners.

By Peter Savage, with foreword by Sir John Egan,
Chairman of Jaguar Cars

Today's winner is without question the company that shows how to utilise the men and women at its disposal more effectively than its competitors can utilise theirs. In *Who Cares Wins*, a practical guidebook to modern management, Peter Savage draws on his own extensive experience to explain how anyone can master the art of group motivation. His step-by-step outline of the key to effective man-management looks at the problems and challenges confronting modern managers and supervisors at every level from the chief executive down, and considers how recent theories of 'excellence' can be transformed into practical and profitable reality.

Savage looks in detail at the right ways and wrong ways of approaching personal relationships at work. He explains how to create a platform for change, then looks at how it can be used, with spectacular results, to unlock unexpected extra energy from colleagues and employees. He identifies this crucial hidden energy as 'discretionary potential' – that piece of ourselves we all take to work but more often than not don't bother to apply. We all know already there are more effective ways of working within organisations large and small: *Who Cares Wins* is the story of how to achieve them.

ISBN 1–85251–070–6   £12.95

COMMON-SENSE BUSINESS STRATEGY

How to improve your profits and cash flow dramatically.

By Barrie Pearson

Millions of managers and business owners have read books or attended seminars on strategy. Few people actually do manage their business strategically and they tend to have become millionaires!

Planning techniques have become so complicated that they are the preserve of 'planning experts'. The result has been long-winded business plans filed and forgotten almost as soon as they have been written.

Successful managers use strategic common-sense, not complex planning techniques. *Common-Sense Business Strategy* shows you how to create your own success story by achieving a 'quantum jump' improvement in results.

This book is based on more than ten years' successful experience of advising businesses ranging from household-name multinationals to unquoted companies and professional partnerships. *Common-Sense Business Strategy* tells you what to do, how to do it, and where to start. It is a book for those who want to manage strategically, and not simply read about it.

Using the techniques he has developed, Barrie Pearson has become an outstandingly successful management consultant and seminar speaker. He is Managing Director of Livingstone Fisher Associates Ltd., Management Consultants, London.

ISBN 1–85251–050–1 £12.95